One of us will come in
tomorrow afternoon to do
hand bills, about 2.30. if you can
be at the top of Morrab Rd.
we should like to see you.
We have sold 6. tickets —

*Note from one of the organisers to a Penzance helper,
and reprinted from the bottom of the poster pictured
on the back cover of this book.*

FRIENDS AND VISITORS:

HISTORY OF THE WOMEN'S SUFFRAGE MOVEMENT IN CORNWALL, 1870-1914

KATHERINE BRADLEY

The Hypatia Trust
Newmill, Penzance, Cornwall

First published 2000 by The Patten Press for The Hypatia Trust
©Katherine Bradley & The Hypatia Trust

Typeset in-house at the Patten Press, Newmill.
Printed in Great Britain at the The Book Factory, London.

ISBN 1 872229 38 7
Women of Cornwall Monograph Series, *The Hypatia Notebooks*

Others in this series:
The Bronte Sisters and Sir Humphry Davy: A sharing of visions (1994)
Kerrow Hill

'Wives, Mothers and Sisters': Feminism, Literature and Women Writers in Cornwall (1998) Alan Kent

CONTENTS

Acknowledgements

This study has taken two years to research and write and I have relied on the friendship, support and advice of numerous people. In particular I would like to thank Melissa Hardie and Andrew Symons (the Jamieson Library) and Professor Angela John for their encouragement and advice. I would also like to thank Gary Tregidga (The Institute of Cornish Studies) and Jo Mattingley for their help and Richard and Caroline Legg and Lisa and Malcolm Grey for their hospitality in Cornwall.

Many staff in numerous libraries have been helpful, in particular the librarians of the Fawcett Library, London, the Bodleian Library, Oxford and the Courtney Library, Truro. Finally, but by no means I would like to thank my husband, Richard, who has given me a great deal of constructive advice and ensured that I persevered with writing up this research.

Abbreviations

CC *Common Cause*
EWR *The Englishwoman's Review*
NLOWS National League for Opposing Women's Suffrage
NUWSS National Union of Women's Suffrage Societies
SU *The Suffragette*
VW *Votes for Women*
WFL Women's Freedom League
WSPU Women's Social and Political Union
WSJ *The Women's Suffrage Journal*

FIRST PHASE OF WOMEN'S SUFFRAGE CAMPAIGN IN CORNWALL.

1855 Langham Place Group
1865 Kensington Society
1866 First women's suffrage petition presented to Parliament. It included two Cornish women signatories.
1867 National Society for Women's suffrage
1869 John Stuart Mill's Book 'The Subjection of Women' published
1871 (February) First suffrage meetings held in Cornwall, Mrs Ronniger - speaker; followed by Miss Beedy(1873); Miss Craigen(1875); Miss Blackburn (1881, 1882 and 1884); Mrs Scatcherd (1882); Miss Wilkinson(1885); and Walter Mclaren, M.P.
1872 First women School Board Members elected in Cornwall (1894 = 7), followed by the election of women Poor Law Guardians (1894 = 25)
1872 The Falmouth Committee for Women's Suffrage
1889 'The Declaration in Favour of Women's Suffrage' included 17 Cornish women signatories
1892 Falmouth committee established to organize and participate in national petition for women's suffrage. They collected 2,830 signatures

SECOND PHASE OF WOMEN'S SUFFRAGE
CAMPAIGN IN CORNWALL.
1897 National Union for Women's
Suffrage Societies (NUWSS)

1903 Women's Social and Political Union
(WSPU)

1909 (March) Launch of WSPU in Penzance
by Annie Kenney; (August) First WSPU
holiday campaign centred in St. Ives

1910 (February) First NUWSS branch
launched in Liskeard by Helen Fraser;
(March) Falmouth NUWSS; Launch of South
Western Federation of the NUWSS;
(December) Falmouth WSPU branch

1911 (March) Penzance NUWSS

1912 (May) Wadebridge NUWSS; (November)
Truro NUWSS; St.Ives NUWSS

1913 (March) Newquay WSPU; (April)
Saltash NUWSS; (June) NUWSS Pilgrimage
Land's End to London; (October)
Launceston NUWSS

1914 (July) Newquay NUWSS.
(August) War declared. NUWSS continued
activity; WSPU disappeared.

1918 Representation of the People Act.

Introduction: setting the scene

'On Tuesday, a lecture was delivered by Mrs Ronniger, delegate from the Women's Rights Association, in the Town Hall, on women's suffrage... to an appreciative audience of about two to three hundred... She spoke and defended women's capability to think rightly on laws relating to marriage, the guardianship of children, education and taxation...fifty and sixty persons signed the petition to Parliament, for single women householders and taxpayers.'
Royal Cornwall Gazette, February 25th, 1871

Mrs Ronniger, a London suffrage supporter and the speaker at the first suffrage meeting in Truro, was one of a number of supporters who toured the British Isles during the 1870s and 1880s. This meeting, part of a series in Cornwall addressed by Mrs Ronniger, marked the beginning of the history of the women's suffrage campaign in the county. It was similar to gatherings taking place all over the United Kingdom and illustrates that the early campaign was not only concerned with 'the vote', but also with wider issues which affected women's lives.

The women's suffrage campaign was part of a wider struggle to broaden the democratic process in 19th century and early 20th century. Other political groups such as the political reform societies, the Chartists and the Liberals were all involved, and developed their ideas against a background of expanding industrialisation, urbanisation and growing prosperity. Women were beginning to make their voices heard in this struggle, firstly in a supportive role, then more directly by campaigning for specific rights and for women's suffrage. The aim of the suffrage supporters was to gain the right to vote in all elections and thus be in a position to influence policies concerned with their rights. By the 1870s the debate on women's suffrage had become part of the public domain and was to remain so until 1928 when all women were granted the vote.

In 1855 the Langham Place Group, a ladies' discussion group was formed in London. This was followed in 1857 by the establishment of the National Association for the Promotion of Social Sciences and in 1858 by the publication of *The English Woman's Journal*. These provided forums where women's suffrage was discussed. In 1865 a new association called the Kensington Society discussed not only topics related to women's rights, but in 1866 they collected the first petition to Parliament on women's suffrage. This was presented by the Liberal M.P., John Stuart Mill. It was followed in 1867 by a second larger petition as an amendment to the Second Reform Bill, which gave the vote to the urban working class male householder. Like all subsequent petitions and proposed Bills it was rejected.

The publication of John Stuart Mill's *The Subjection of Women* (1869) provided the suffrage movement with a set of intellectual arguments. These were based on the liberal ideals of individual rights, freedom of choice, equality of opportunity and civil liberties. This liberal individualism promised women an equal standing with men. Thus from the 1870s onwards the debate was not just concerned with women's franchise but with other concerns, such as education, property and legal rights and employment.

In 1867, the National Society for Women's Suffrage, a loose federation of women's suffrage groups, was formed. Societies were established in London and some of the main provincial cities, such as Bristol, Birmingham, Edinburgh and Manchester. Many of the early members were middle class, often non-conformist women and men who had been involved in earlier pressure groups such as the Anti-Slavery movement and the Anti-Corn Law League. They adopted these earlier organisations' campaigning methods, that is, they petitioned and lobbied Parliament and M.P.s, held public meetings and worked together with pro-suffrage M.P.s. Their actions were law abiding and their case carefully argued.

Their aim was to establish the right of women to be heard and to persuade male opinion of the justice of their cause. They argued that women should be given the same voting rights as men and on the same basis of property rights. However, by 1874 divisions emerged. To begin with some members supported the view that only spinsters and widows should be given the vote, whilst others supported the enfranchisement of married women. In the 1880s the debate gathered momentum as a result of the Third Reform Act in 1884 which gave many agricultural workers the vote, whilst propertied women could not vote. As a result the Women's Franchise League was formed that same year. It campaigned for married women with property to be given the vote. At the same time the Central Committee for the National Society for Women's Suffrage was formed to support voting rights for single women and widows. In 1888 a further division appeared when a breakaway group from the Central Committee decided to align itself to the Women's Liberal Federation (the Central National Committee for Women's Suffrage). Finally in 1891 one other group emerged. This was the Women's Emancipation Union, a breakaway group from the Women's Franchise League. They argued that women should be granted the vote in stages.

By the early 1900s, the two main groups, the National Union for Women's Suffrage Societies (NUWSS) - formed in 1897 as a federation of the existing societies - and the Women's Social and Political Union (WSPU), campaigned for all women to have the vote, regardless of their marital status. Instead arguments and divisions were more concerned with the tactics in achieving women's suffrage, although the debate about whether to be allied to a political party or not remained controversial. It is against these political developments that the debate on women's suffrage took place all over Britain.

Cornwall, particularly Falmouth through the Quaker Fox family, had early connections with the suffrage movement. The Foxes were acquainted with John Stuart Mill and members of the Bright family and other Quaker.families involved in the campaign. This local family and their friends, together with a series of visiting speakers, played a pivotal role in the development of the suffrage movement ensuring that there was continuity of support throughout its history.

Cornwall, 1870-1914

In order to understand the Cornish women's suffrage movement, a brief description of Cornwall during this period is necessary. Many outsiders, including historians, perceive 19th century and early 20th century Cornwall as a predominantly rural county, although much has been written by a variety of Cornish historians to counteract this perception. In fact, Cornwall was among the first counties to become industrialised. By the mid-19th century, as a result of the early application of steam operated machinery, the economy was dominated by tin mining, which between 1852 and 1913 contributed 99% of Britain's production. Mines also produced copper, lead, zinc, iron ore and silver accounting for 50% of Britain's non-ferrous metal production. Allied to this industry was the development of engineering. However on the downside, the periodic slumps and gradual decline in mining resulted in massive emigration to other areas of Britain and to British colonies. This meant that unlike other parts of Britain the population declined from 369,390 in 1861 to 322,320 in 1901 (Payton 1992; 1993).

Evidence of the mining industry litters the Cornish landscape and many of the small towns and villages, such as Redruth, Camborne, Pendeen and St. Just owed their development to this industry. Mining was also responsible for the improvement of local communications including the development of railways. The Cornish economy gradually became marginalised in spite of other important economic activities such as pilchard fishing, china clay, agriculture and tourism. Tourism, of course, was helped by the introduction of the railways and the attraction of the mild climate and beautiful scenery. Penzance became a major resort and new tourist destinations developed such as St. Ives and Newquay. There was, however, an absence of large towns. The three largest towns according to the 1911 census were Penzance (13,474), Falmouth (13,172) and Truro (11,372). Thus by the end of the 19th century Cornwall consisted of a scattered collection of small towns and villages.

Religion was an important influence on Cornish social and political life. As the 1851 census illustrated, mining communities were dominated by Methodism, mainly through the influence of the Wesleyan Association and the Bible Christians. By the end of the 19th century, however, their support was declining. Unlike other Methodist areas there was no strong labour movement, and Cornish Methodism was primarily concerned with individual self-improvement. It was closely associated with the development of a large Temperance movement, as well as a number of educational, literary and improving societies. With the purposes of counteracting Methodist influence, the Church of England established a new diocese in Truro in 1876 and built a new cathedral there in the 1880s.

Mining was also responsible for the expansion of the middle classes, families who had either made small fortunes through the industry or who were involved in developing the infrastructure of the county, such as the Fox family in Falmouth. Some landowners also made their fortunes through their ownership of mines, for example the Trevelyans and St. Aubyns. Both groups contributed to the cultural and political life of the county, as patrons of the arts and sciences, establishing institutions such as the Royal Cornwall Polytechnic Society in Falmouth (1833) and in the 1850s, the Launceston Philosophical Society and the St. Austell Useful Knowledge Society.

Towards the end of the century an articulate minority in Cornwall, were attempting to establish a specific Cornish identity. This Cornish revival ushered in a renewed interest in the Cornish language, Celtic mythology and a romantic vision of Cornwall before industrialisation. This was aided and abetted by the production of contemporary guide books which stressed the romantic landscape forged by Celtic and Arthurian shrines such as the one at Tintagel.

Politically, Cornwall was dominated by the Liberal party. By 1885 all the constituencies returned Liberal or Liberal Unionist MPs. The County Council, established in the new county town of Truro in 1889, was dominated by the Liberals and Liberal Unionists. Perhaps a more important political development for middle class women, was the possibility that they could now contribute to local politics. Nationally from 1870 they could be elected as School Board members, from 1875 as Poor Law Guardians, and from 1894 as Parish and District Councillors. Cornwall had two of the first female School Board members in 1872 and by 1894 there were approximately seven School Board members and twenty-five Poor Law Guardians (EWR 1891-1902; Hollis 1987; Metcalfe 1917). Some of these women were also members of the suffrage movement.

The most important was Miss Frances Sterling (1869-1943), the first female Poor Law Guardian to be elected in Falmouth in 1891. She was born in London, the daughter of Edward and Bertha Sterling (Crawford 1999; *NUWSS Annual Reports* 1904-1918). Her family, particularly her mother, supported women's suffrage. Her grandfather was the poet John Sterling, and a close friend of the Fox family. This might explain her presence in Falmouth, since the family was based in London. She may also have owned property nearby at Budock Rural (*Kelly's Directory*, 1910). She inherited her mother's artistic ability and specialised in genre painting, exhibiting at the Royal Academy between 1881 and 1900. She gave up painting in 1902 in order to work full time for the suffrage movement, both as an executive committee member of the London Society for Women's Suffrage and the NUWSS and as a travelling speaker. Eventually, from 1903 until 1909, she was joint honorary secretary of the NUWSS and in 1913, President of the Falmouth branch of the NUWSS. She was a both a Quaker and a Liberal and a founder member of the Falmouth Women's Liberal Association. She continued to support women's rights until her death.

There were other Poor Law Guardians who supported women's suffrage, for example, Miss Lillie Paull, elected in Truro in 1895. Later in 1905, Miss Olivia Lloyd Fox, the secretary of Falmouth NUWSS, was elected. The only Cornish School Board member to support suffrage was Mrs M. Dungey, a member of the Redruth School Board in 1894. By 1900, five Cornish women were elected members of Rural District Councils. For example, in Truro, Lillie Paull and a Miss Elliott were members of the local Rural Highways Committee.

With the development of women's political associations, women were also able to participate in party politics. By the late 1880s Cornish women participated in the Primrose League and established branches of the Women's Liberal Federation, the Women's Liberal Association and the Women's Liberal Unionist Association.

Researching the Cornish Women's Suffrage Movement

In order to gain a clear understanding of the Cornish suffrage movement I have divided its history into two phases. The first phase began in 1871 and continued into the 1890s. The second phase began in 1909, when first the Women's Social and Political Union (WSPU) began an intensive campaign, closely followed by the National Union of Women's Suffrage Societies (NUWSS). Activity continued until the advent of the First World War when the WSPU disappeared and the NUWSS turned its attention to supporting the war effort and survived until 1918. Throughout both phases there was a lively debate on women's suffrage in Cornwall, not that dissimilar to much of the national debate, although as I will illustrate, there were also some important differences.

A number of factors were important in the development of the suffrage movement in Cornwall. These include the political and religious make up of the County as well as its economic and social structure. Particularly important were the emerging liberal middle classes that were the largest groups to support women's suffrage, as they were nationally. Thus as already noted, 19th and early 20th century Cornwall was not the backwater often assumed by historians and contemporary commentators, but an outward looking society which by the turn of the century was becoming gradually more cosmopolitan. To an extent this is demonstrated by the debates on women's suffrage led by a mixture of 'insiders' and a number of 'outsiders', that is, visiting suffrage speakers and organisers, who periodically toured the County during both phases of suffrage activity.

This study is an analysis of the development of the Cornish suffrage movement: its connections with the national movement; the differences and similarities between Cornish membership and activities with other local societies outside London and the major provincial cities, and the contributions made by Cornish suffrage supporters to local politics. Thus the material is presented both chronologically and thematically. It is based on an analysis of the national suffrage journals and their annual reports, as well as local newspapers. Other material used includes Cornish histories, the histories of the national movement, *The Englishwoman's Review* and *The Women's Who's Who*, all of which provide some of the biographical material (see bibliography).

As a result I have been able to reconstruct a large part of the history of the Cornish movement and identify some of its supporters and activists. This includes the 'visitors' and some of the local figures. However, material about local activists and supporters has proved exceptionally difficult to discover because unless individuals have contributed to the national movement or played a major role locally, few biographical details have survived. Also as other historians of the suffrage movement outside London have found, local supporters have on the whole remained marginalised. For example, as long ago as 1977, the historian Jill Liddington, who together with Jill Norris, was embarking on a study of women's suffrage in Lancashire, commented (Liddington 1977, 192)

'In the usual versions of the suffrage histories, the focus centres on London, and the activists are predominantly middle-class suffragettes led by the Pankhursts. The process of uncovering this kind of local story has inevitably been haphazard. Occasionally it was frustrating, frequently rewarding.'

Although her book *One Hand Tied Behind Us* was written over twenty years ago, the majority of studies written since have continued to concentrate on the national movement; and are centred on London and the second phase of the movement, particularly the suffragettes. Gradually a few historians have extended their research to some of the major provincial cities, Scotland and to a lesser extent Wales. However all have been faced with similar difficulties, for example, David Neville in his recent study of the women's suffrage movement in North East England (Neville 1998). A few more recent studies, such as Sandra Holton's *Suffrage Days* (1996) have concentrated on the more peripheral groups and lesser-known activists.

16

The reason for these problems is not because there is a shortage of material, but that the piecing together of this information is more complicated than for London, or even Manchester, where major archival resources exist. In the more rural areas where fewer records have survived and where lesser-known women campaigned for suffrage, it is particularly difficult to reconstruct the membership.

Cornwall is therefore a challenging county in which to uncover women's history, since the archives are scattered and until recently local historians have shown little interest in women's contribution to its past. Biographies and autobiographies of women writers and artists, such as Daphne Du Maurier and Laura Knight exist. However it is only in the last few years that women have been included in the histories of the art colonies, and even more recently (1998) that the first study on relatively unknown Cornish women writers by Alan Kent has appeared, as commissioned by the Hypatia Trust.

So why choose Cornwall? As an annual visitor in recent years to the southern part of the county, I became fascinated by its history and especially with the lack of an overt women's literature. As I visited museums and art galleries I was struck by the many visual images of women often painted by women during this period. As a result I initially thought that one of the major characteristics of the Cornish suffrage movement would be the membership of women artists, those living and working in the artists' colonies of south west Cornwall. This was reinforced by my reading of various books on women artists, such as *Painting Women* (Cherry 1995, 93) in which Cherry argues that 'Women artists contributed to the campaigns for votes for women... As respectable professionals, women artists embodied many of the arguments for the greater public activity and responsibility of women. From the launch of the suffrage movement in the 1860s they joined suffrage societies, gave money, spoke at meetings, turned their studios and dwellings into campaign centres, and signed petitions.'

Indeed one of the founders of the suffrage movement and also an artist, did visit Cornwall and bought a house at Zennor near St. Ives (Hirsch 1998, 284). This was Barbara Leigh Smith Bodichon (1827-1891) who in 1874 first visited friends who lived at 'Eagles' Nest',

Zennor. She became so fascinated by the rugged coastal landscape that she returned again and eventually bought the parish poor house from the Penzance Union in July 1875. She stayed there until October 1877 when she was forced to return to London after a stroke. Her original intention had been to establish an artist's haven in Zennor. This wish was not fulfilled until after her death when she left the house to her friend, the gardener, Gertrude Jekyll. The house then was used by various women artists including some from the Newlyn colony of artists. However Barbara Bodichon did not have contact with any of the Cornish suffrage supporters during her stay in Cornwall. Other painters on the periphery of the Cornish movement are mentioned later.

Another reason for thinking that women artists would be involved in suffrage activity is that much of the later campaign was based on visual propaganda. In London two groups, the Suffrage Atelier and the Artist's Suffrage League, together with Sylvia Pankhurst, contributed to this. However, after a great deal of research, with the help of the Jamieson Library, which also shelters the West Cornwall Art Archive, I found that few women artists living and working in Cornwall contributed to the propaganda and seemingly were not engaged with this issue in their work. Thus an interest in art did not form the bond that I had envisaged. I suspect that the reason for this was because they were more preoccupied with earning a living and establishing their artistic reputations. Instead I found a movement that was dominated by a network of mainly middle class 'visitors' and 'friends' and that there was virtually no use made of visual material in Cornwall.

It is against this background that I will now examine the first phase of the Cornish suffrage movement.

Laying the Foundations: the first stepping stones in the campaign for women's suffrage, 1870-1900

'I am reading that terrible book of John Mill's *On Liberty*, so clear and calm, and cold... He looks you through like a basilisk, relentless as Fate. We knew him well at one time, and owe him very much; I fear his remorseless logic has led him far since then.'
The Journals of Caroline Fox 1835-1871.

Caroline Fox wrote this in her diary in September, 1859 (Monk 1972, 229). *On Liberty*, just published, was one of the most influential books on liberal democracy and the forerunner of *The Subjection of Women*, on which Caroline made no comment. Earlier in 1839, the Mill family had moved to Falmouth just after the death of James Mill. Like many visitors they were attracted by its mild climate. Mrs Mill and her two daughters spent their time in Falmouth nursing their youngest brother, Henry, who was dying from tuberculosis. There, the family was visited by John, a close friend of John Sterling, and through him met the Fox family. Later Mill and the Foxes met in London, although by the 1850s the friendship was fading.

The Foxes were wealthy Quakers who had settled in Cornwall in the 18th century. They were highly educated, well travelled and were related to other leading Quakers, such as the Fry, Gurney and Sturge families, all of whom were suffrage supporters. This provided them with a large network of friends and relatives and enabled them to keep in close touch with liberal politics. The family business was shipping, G. C. Fox & Sons (which still exists) and they had interests in mining, fishing and engineering. All were interested in the arts and sciences and were friends of leading politicians, scientists, writers and artists.

Caroline (1819-1871) and Anna Fox (1815-1896), the daughters of Robert Were Fox and Maria Barclay, were two remarkable women. In 1833 they helped establish the Royal Cornwall Polytechnic Society (an idea of Anna's) with the aim of promoting education, art, science, commerce and manufacturing. Anna painted and was active in promoting the arts. Two close relatives, Howard and Blanche Fox were also involved in the suffrage movement. He chaired early suffrage meetings and she was secretary of the Falmouth suffrage committee in 1872. The next generation of the family as well as some of their friends, also played an important part in the movement, as will be described later. This was unlike the majority of other activists who tended to participate solely either in the early or later period of the movement.

In February 1871 the first public meetings on women's suffrage were held. Mrs Ronniger, (mentioned in the Introduction) "well-known for her talented readings, gave lectures on women's suffrage in many towns in Cornwall" (*WSJ* March 1871). During her week's visit she addressed crowded meetings in six Cornish towns, beginning at the small town of Helston and then travelling to Truro, Bodmin, Lanceston, Falmouth and finally Liskeard. At the end of November that year she returned to Cornwall and this time visited Falmouth, Truro, Liskeard and Helston. Both visits were organised by the London National Society for Women's Suffrage.

In March 1873 a second suffrage visitor to Cornwall was Miss Beedy, M.A., an American graduate from Vassar College. She gave a series of lectures on women's suffrage, first at Penzance to an audience of 700, followed by crowded meetings at Camborne, Penryn, Helston, Truro, St Austell and Redruth, and then continued her tour in Dorset. The following December she returned to Penzance to address a meeting of 600 people, then continued to Truro and Liskeard. These meetings followed a similar format. For example, at the Liskeard meeting, Miss Beedy spoke for an hour. This was followed by a resolution to send a petition to Parliament, proposed by a Mr Saunders and seconded by the Reverend J. Simpson. It was passed unanimously. In Truro she (*WSJ* January 1875) 'expressed her satisfaction in receiving support everywhere she visited in Cornwall. In only two instances did she meet a gentleman opposed to women's suffrage.'

Public meetings during this first phase of suffrage activity in Cornwall were similar to those held throughout the country, the format only slightly changing during the second phase when meetings were organised by women. The majority of meetings were held in central public halls, such as town halls, and speakers addressed large and supportive audiences. They were usually chaired by a local dignitary, such as the Lord Mayor, a local Anglican or Non-conformist clergyman, or a professional or businessman and were supported by a large platform party.

The third visiting speaker was the eccentric Miss Jessie Craigen, a Scottish woman who travelled throughout Britain with her dog 'Tiny'. In October 1875, she travelled from Exeter to Cornwall to address meetings in the more remote rural and working class areas. She spoke at the Mechanic's Institute in Looe and at the Mount Zion Methodist Chapel, Mousehole, a fishing village near Penzance, as well as addressing open-air meetings in mining villages (*WSJ* December 1875).

By the 1880s all the public meetings were addressed by speakers from the Bristol and West of England Society for Women's Suffrage, which had been established in 1868. *The Women's Suffrage Journal* again records the visits of these speakers and the meetings.

The first visitor, Miss Helen Blackburn, the Society's secretary, accompanied by Miss Orme, addressed two meetings at Penzance and Truro, in the autumn of 1881. She then returned to Cornwall three more times. The following year, she was accompanied by Miss Emily Spender, a member from Bath. They addressed three meetings. Then later on in 1882 she gave a lecture to the St. Austell Liberal Debating Society. Finally in mid-January, 1884, she returned again with Emily Spender, to address three meetings. All these meetings were well supported.

At the end of 1882, yet another visiting speaker, Mrs Alice Scatcherd, a suffrage supporter from Yorkshire, came to give a lecture at Launceston. She was specifically invited by a Mrs Banbury (*WSJ* January 1883) and might have been on holiday, since unlike the other speakers she did not address a series of meetings.

Finally in March 1885, the last female visiting speaker, Miss Wilkinson, an early woman trade unionist, toured the West Country, including Cornwall. During her fortnight's visit she addressed eight meetings, all apparently well received as the following comment illustrates (*EWR* March 1885) "Miss Wilkinson is an able and eloquent speaker, and everyone who has once heard her is anxious to hear her again." At St. Austell the title for her talk, "If the vote is good for Jack, why not for Jill?", was a little more inspiring than most. At Liskeard she was the guest of the local Liberal Association, the first political association to officially discuss women's suffrage in Cornwall.

The last of the visiting speakers was Mr Walter Mclaren, a Parliamentary supporter, who addressed the Launceston and Truro Liberal Associations in January 1890. His talks were on a slightly different subject, the influence of women in politics rather than women's suffrage (EWR February 1890). For the first time, the initial meeting of the series was chaired by a woman, Mrs Dungey.

Thus by 1890 meetings had been organised in all the main centres of Cornwall, as well as some in the smaller villages. The most popular town to be visited was Truro, followed by Liskeard, Redruth, Helston and Bodmin. All these meetings followed a similar pattern to the one already described. In almost all cases there was surprisingly no opposition and resolutions to send a petition to Parliament were passed unanimously. Instead, opposition was voiced by some of the local M.P.s and at other meetings.

From 1870 until the 1890s Parliament was bombarded with local and national petitions in support of the bills proposed annually by M.P.s. The remoter areas of Britain like Cornwall also received visits from a number of visiting speakers, usually on behalf of the largest nearby suffrage society, unless there were members able to speak and organise meetings in their own towns.

So who were these visiting speakers? Apart from Alice Scatcherd and Eliza Orme, they belonged to a group of about fifteen intrepid women who travelled throughout Britain to promote women's suffrage as widely as possible (Mason, 1912, 51). All were acquainted with each other and campaigned for a variety of issues concerned with women's rights and were well known public speakers. Surprisingly they came from a variety of backgrounds, both middle and working class. Indeed Mrs Ronniger, Jessie Craigen and possibly Jeanette Wilkinson were 'peripatetic employees' (Crawford, 1999, 474-479) in that unlike the majority of members who gave their time and services voluntarily, they were paid, probably because they had no private income.

There is scant information about Miss Beedy, but it has been relatively easy to discover details about the other visiting speakers, since *The Englishwoman's Review* published detailed obituaries. In addition Sandra Holton in *Suffrage Days* has written about Jessie Craigen and Alice Scatcherd; Olive Banks about Helen Blackburn in *The Biographical Dictionary of British Feminists* and very recently Elizabeth Crawford has written about them all in *The Women's Suffrage Movement*. All, as will be shown, were quite remarkable and accomplished women and deserve a great deal more attention than they have hitherto been given.

The first speaker, Mrs. or Madame M. Jane Ronniger (?-?1892) lived in London, where in 1865 she was a member of the Kensington Society. She then joined the London National Society for Women's Suffrage in 1868/9 and in 1871 the Manchester Society. However it was under the auspices of the London Society, who possibly paid her, that she travelled the country, including Cornwall. As indicated by the *Royal Cornwall Gazette*, (February 4th, 1871) "she gave dramatic and poetic readings at the Concert Hall" in Truro. In fact she was a teacher of voice and recitation and gave lectures and readings at provincial literary societies. She also wrote songs, painted portraits that were exhibited at the Female Art Institute in 1879 and was the editor of the *Aesthetic Review* and *Art Observer* between 1879 and 1880.

The second visitor Miss Mary Beedy, M.A. was an American suffragist (Mason, 1912, 51) "whose practical commonsense and clear logic made her advocacy invaluable" and "who charmed even her opponents by her amiability" (Mason, 1912, 56). Audiences were puzzled by the title M.A., since English women in the early 1870s were not awarded university degrees. She was an early graduate of Vassar College, the first women's college in the United States (1865) to offer women degrees. Here she taught and wrote on women's education. In 1872 she travelled to Ireland and Wales and in 1873 to the West of England.

Much more is known about the third speaker, Miss Jessie Craigen (1834? - 1899). She came from an unlikely background for a suffrage speaker at this time. She was the daughter of an Italian actress and a Scottish ship's captain who died when she was still a child. Jessie was trained by her mother for the stage and began her public life at the age of four, as a pantomime fairy. By 1870 she left the stage to participate in public life to lecture on temperance and helped to form a trade union in Scotland. By 1873 she began to tour the country as a public speaker on women's suffrage. She planned her own tours and was the first woman suffragist to address outdoor meetings. Before each meeting she would send a bell ringer round with a few suffrage notices to announce the meeting (*EWR*, January 1900)

'and quickly that powerful voice drew crowds around her. Amongst the miners in Cornwall, the agricultural labourers of Dorsetshire, the colliers of South Wales, the factory hands of Lancashire and Yorkshire, the miners of Durham and the north, she seemed equally at home.'

At each meeting she would collect signatures for petitions and send a bundle of these "very genuine and very dirty" papers to Lydia Becker or Miss Ashworth (*EWR* January 1900). Because of her poverty, she was one of the few women to be financed periodically by the suffrage societies or individual members. By 1886 her work and attitude towards women's suffrage was considered to be rather quixotic and radical and she had to work under a manager. By the mid-1880s she was also involved in working for the Irish Land League and for the Ladies' National Association for the repeal of the Contagious Diseases Acts, gradually abandoning the suffrage cause. She died in poverty in Ilford, Essex. From comments made in *The Suffrage Journal* and elsewhere, it seems that the majority of leading suffragists only just tolerated this large, ungainly and badly dressed woman, as the last part of her obituary illustrates (EWR January 1900):

'Poor Jessie Craigen, hers was a life 'Dark through excess of light': her passionate craving for justice and for affection blinded her to the true ways of obtaining either on this side of the grave. Peace be to her memory.'

She was followed by one of the most influential and indefatigable suffrage workers, Miss Helen Blackburn (1842-1903). Helen was born on Valentia Island, Ireland, the only surviving daughter of a civil engineer and inventor and his wife. In 1859 the family moved to London where she spent most of her time painting watercolour landscapes until the age of twenty-two or three when she had to give this up due to her deteriorating eyesight. It was at this time that she began to contribute articles to *The Englishwoman's Review*, eventually becoming its editor in 1890. Between 1874 and 1877 she was Secretary of the Central Committee of the National Society for Women's Suffrage.

Helen remained a member of its executive committee and in 1880 combined this role with that of secretary of the Bristol and West of England Women's Suffrage Society. Here in 1885 she organised an Exhibition of Women's Industries and used her artistic skills to design the catalogue. Also in Bristol together with the suffrage committee, £1,000 was raised, which was used to enact her (*EWR* April 1903) "... systematic plans of work throughout the Western Counties and South Wales during the next three years." This probably funded her visits to Cornwall. She wrote a great deal on women's rights. Her two most important books were *A Handbook for Women Engaged in Social and Political Work* (1881) and *Women's Suffrage: A Record of the Movement in the British Isles* (1902).

In 1895 she retired from most of her suffrage activity to look after her elderly father in London. She did however find time to take on the position of joint secretary of the London Central Association together with Millicent Fawcett. Shortly after her father's death she formed the Freedom of Labour Defence Association (*EWR* April 1903)
'...to protect workers especially women workers, from such restrictive legislation as lessens their wage-earning capacity, limits their personal liberty, and inconveniences them in their private lives.'

In 1899 she attended her last suffrage meeting, the annual meeting in Bristol. That year her health began to deteriorate and she was forced to confine her activities to editing *The Englishwoman's Review* and continued this until her death. Judging by the many obituaries cited in that journal in 1903, Helen Blackburn had a great many friends and was greatly admired not only for all her hard work and devotion to the cause but for her 'unfailing courtesy' and 'her never-failing kindness.'

Her two companions, Emily Spender and Eliza Orme, were not only friends but early suffrage supporters and well-known for other activities. Emily Spender (1841-1922), a novelist, was the first secretary of the Bath Committee of the National Society for Women's Suffrage in 1871. Eliza (Elizabeth) Orme was the secretary of the London National Society for Women's Suffrage in 1871. In the 1870s she attempted to enter the legal profession and eventually became a legal conveyancer. She was a moderate member of the Women's Liberal Federation and in 1892 joined the Women's National Liberal Association, editing their journal, *The Women's Gazette*. As well as writing for *The Englishwoman's Review* and *Nineteenth Century*, she campaigned for prison reform, in particular the removal of some female criminals from prison to hospital and in 1893 led a team of four Lady Assistant Commissioners employed by the Royal Commission of Labour to investigate women's employment.

As a campaigner, Alice Scatcherd (1842-1906) was known for being an outspoken and radical suffrage supporter, a Liberal activist and campaigner for a variety of women's causes. She was the wife of a wealthy textile manufacturer and a friend of the Pankhurst family and a great favourite with the Pankhurst children. Sylvia Pankhurst described her as (Pankhurst 1977, 97)

'...a tall, bony Yorkshire woman of Morley, near Leeds, of substantial means and assured social position she repudiated as badges of slavery, and refused to wear either a wedding ring or the veil with which the well-dressed woman covered her face in those days.'

At first her suffrage activity was fairly orthodox. She was a member of the Manchester Society for Women's Suffrage. She then helped to launch the breakaway radical Women's Franchise League, which was led by Mrs Wolstonholme Elmy, and was its treasurer until it disbanded in 1897. In the 1870s and 1880s she supported working women, including a weavers' strike. In the suffrage movement she helped to organise demonstrations and petitions.

The final member of this group, Miss Jeanette Gaury Wilkinson (1842-1886), was the daughter of a foreman of a large warehouse in London. From the age of seventeen she earned her living as an upholsterer, eventually combining this with studying at evening classes at Birkbeck Institute. Although she did not complete her studies, they enabled her to work in a Board school in Southwark between 1877 and 1879. She then left to take up other teaching jobs until she was appointed Secretary of the National Vigilance Society. After that she became one of the organising secretaries for the Bristol and West of England Women's Suffrage Society, working together with Helen Blackburn. In 1885 she returned to London to help organise meetings for the Central Committee of the National Society for Women's Suffrage.

Jeanette Wilkinson addressed numerous public meetings in London and elsewhere. Apart from her suffrage work she was also active in the women's trade union movement and the Liberal Party. She was a member of the Society of Upholsteresses and spoke as a delegate to the TUC on conditions in workshops. Then in 1884 and 1885 she brought up the issue of women's suffrage, where she won TUC support in spite of bitter opposition. As an executive committee member of her local Liberal Association she addressed public meetings in support of Home Rule. As her obituary commented (*EWR* September 1886):

'Her manner was pleasant and cheery at all times. Her small body never seemed strong enough for the tasks she set it to do, but the bright eye and determined mouth showed where the strength came from to supply physical deficiencies... She spoke impressively, saying what she wished to say in short, pithy sentences, and never lulling her audiences to sleep with musical platitudes. Every sentence was needed in the chain of logical argument and therefore every sentence was listened to. It is probable that her training as a teacher did much to improve her skill as a lecturer.'

She died at home from a severe attack of bronchitis. A memorial fund was set up which paid for her niece to attend a girls' school in Falmouth. The treasurer of that fund was Helen Blackburn.

The one male visiting speaker, Walter Mclaren (1853-1912), an Independant Liberal M.P., was the youngest son of Priscilla Bright, the younger sister of John Bright; and Duncan Mclaren, M.P. for Edinburgh, both early suffrage supporters. He was educated and brought up in Edinburgh where he attended university. He then went into business in Keighley and joined the worsted spinning firm, Smith and McLaren. He retired the year he visited Cornwall, although he remained a director of an important coal and iron company. In 1886 he married Eva Muller. He was twice M.P. for Crewe (1886-1895 and 1910-1912). Throughout his political life he supported not only women's suffrage, but also Free Trade and Home Rule, addressing many public meetings on these issues.

It has proved difficult to discover who issued the invitations to these visiting speakers, who the local activists were and whether there were other suffrage activities in the county apart from public meetings. The reports of the public meetings do however give some of the names of those present, particularly those of the chairman, and the proposers and seconders of the resolutions for sending local petitions to Parliament. There are also a few other helpful clues. These include suffrage petitions and subscription lists that record the addresses of signatories and subscribers; and local reports of political meetings, particularly during election periods.

The public meetings were 'presided' over by a dignitary. These included the Reverend W. Roberts (Bodmin, 1871), local magistrates, for example Mr Jacob Oliver (Falmouth. 1871 and 1872), Mr Thomas Solomon (Truro, 1875) and Mr Cardell (Bodmin, 1885) or the mayor or the chairman of the School Board or tradesmen. They were probably all leading Liberals. They were supported on the platform by a group of dignitaries. Similarly resolutions were proposed and seconded by men with similar backgrounds, who were all used to speaking in public. This format was used in the majority of political public meetings throughout the 19th century and only began to change when women became more confident of speaking in public (Shiman 1992). A brief report in *The Women's Suffrage Journal* (February 1884) describes a typical suffrage meeting:

'A meeting on behalf of the enfranchisement of women was held in the large room of the Board Schools, St. Ives, on 17th January. Mr W. Craze, J.P., presided and there was also on the platform the Rev. A. Colbeck, Messrs. Anthony, J. Daniell, and Niunis [sic]. The room was crowded to excess. The Chairman briefly explained the object of the meeting. Miss Blackburn and Miss Spender then addressed the meeting, after which the Rev. A. Colbeck moved a resolution in support of the principle and the adoption of a petition and memorial to the member for the borough. This was seconded by Mr Morgan Anthony. On its being put to the meeting a large number of hands were held up in its favour and not one against.'

The printed suffrage parliamentary petitions during the 19th century indicate that there was Cornish support from the earliest petition in 1866 until at least 1897. The first suffrage petition included two Falmouth women, Mrs Howard Fox, later the secretary of the Falmouth Society, and Miss Hockin, who lived in the same road as the Fox family, Wood Lane.

Table 1. The Falmouth Committee for Women's Suffrage, 1872.
Source: *The Women's Suffrage Journal*, February 1872.

Mr William Cornish	Rev R. C. Moses
Mr J. P. Cregon	Mr Jacob Oliver, J.P.
Mr E. B. Eastwick, M.P.	Mrs Edward Read
Mr R. N. Fowler, M.P.	Mr Frederick Renfrew
Mrs Genn	Mrs Joseph Sheddon
Miss Krabbe	

Honorary Secretary: Mrs Howard Fox

In 1872 a municipal petition to Parliament to support the *1872 Disabilities Removal Act* was signed by Falmouth Council, the only Cornish Council to support it. This indicates that Falmouth suffrage supporters were a powerful lobby in the town. In fact it coincides with the formation of a short-lived suffrage committee (see Table 1). During this period Falmouth was unusual in having such a committee since only the large provincial cities and London had societies and a few important smaller cities such as Bath, had formal groups.

This was mainly as a result of their radical tradition or because articulate, often non-conformist supporters, organised these groups. The latter accounts for the Falmouth group. Here at the beginning of 1872 a women's suffrage committee was formed which was affiliated to the Central Committee of the National Society for Women's Suffrage. Although it is difficult to ascertain how long this survived, it organised a number of meetings in Falmouth and the nearby town of Penryn during 1872 and 1873. The Committee consisted of five women and seven men. Male members included one clergyman, the Reverend R. C. Moses, a magistrate, Mr Jacob Oliver who had chaired the first suffrage meeting in February 1871 and the two M.P.s for Falmouth and Penryn from 1868 until 1874, the Conservative-Liberal, Edward Eastwick (1814-1883), and the Conservative, Sir Robert Fowler (1828-1891). The latter might have been a member because he was related through marriage to the Fox family. He was married to Charlotte Fox, the second daughter of Alfred Fox.

Two committee members, Mrs Howard (Blanche) Fox and Mrs Genn (1829-1897), the wife of the town clerk, William Genn (1811-1890) maintained an interest in the issue throughout their lifetime, participating at the very least in signing later parliamentary petitions. This early group also provided continuity with the second phase of women's suffrage since members of the Genn and Fox families were actively involved in the Falmouth NUWSS from 1911 onwards. They were neighbours and friends. In the 1880s and 1890s, the painter Henry Tuke (1858-1929), a neighbour of both families and a Quaker, painted Anna Maria Fox, Howard Fox and William Genn and his wife. The Genns had numerous children, including Julia, who was later active in the NUWSS together with Mrs Ellen Fox and her daughter Naomi and niece Olivia.

In 1889 *'The Declaration in Favour of Women's Suffrage'* included seventeen Cornish women. It was organised in response to the first anti-suffrage 'Women's Manifesto' published in the magazine *Nineteenth Century*, earlier that year. Here the author, Mrs Humphry Ward, requested women to sign a resolution against the extension of the parliamentary franchise to women which 1,200 did. However, the pro-suffrage 'Declaration' was supported by over 2,000 'ladies'. They were grouped under specific headings.These included under 'businesswomen', the postmistress of Launceston, Miss Martha Melhuisk Truscott, and under 'miscellaneous', eleven women from Truro including Miss Lillie Paull; two Penzance women, Mrs Hodgson Pratt, the future secretary of the Penzance branch of the NUWSS and Mrs Henry Sturge who was related to the Sturge family, active supporters in Bristol; and four Falmouth women, including Miss Fox and Mrs Diplock.

Three years later in 1892 the Central Committee of the National Society for Women's Suffrage organised a petition 'An Appeal from Women of All Parties and Classes'. This was planned in a different way to other petitions, in that books for the collection of signatures were circulated and collected by local committees throughout the country and then returned to the central office in London. One such committee was formed in Falmouth. Its secretary was Mrs Lander Eaton and its committee which included Miss Lillie Paull and Leonard Courtney's sister, held meetings in Falmouth, Truro and possibly Bodmin (*EWR* January 1894). They collected 1,304 signatures in Bodmin and 1,526 in Falmouth and Penryn. By 1896 a total of 257,796 signatures were collected from all over the country, the largest petition presented to Parliament since the Chartist ones in the 1840s. In spite of this the Bill failed.

In 1897 the same national committee organised a petition which included over seventy painters including Elizabeth Armstrong Forbes, a leading artist, living and painting in Newlyn. That year this committee was responsible for setting up the NUWSS, since their activity had demonstrated that by working together, the different suffrage groups could mount a coherent national campaign.

Another important clue which indicates local support, comes from suffrage subscription lists, which were published in *The Women's Suffrage Journal*. By 1879, the nearest suffrage society, the Bristol and the West of England Women's Suffrage Society, included three regular Cornish subscribers. The first of these was the Reverend Prebendary Philip Hedgeland, Vicar of St. Mary's Church, Penzance. He was later a Vice President of Penzance NUWSS. On October 12th, 1882 he chaired his first suffrage meeting at St. John's Hall, Penzance. Here he commented (*WSJ* November 1881)

"Never in his life before had he taken the chair of a meeting of a political tendency, but as the politics were social rather than party, he did not think he could be really out of place as a clergyman in holding the present position...He had never been able to see why women should not have a vote for members of Parliament. (Applause) He looked around and saw what sort of men were allowed to vote, and speaking as one who was never an advocate of universal suffrage, it seemed to him that a vast number of men were entrusted with the suffrage who could hardly safely be entrusted with it, but everywhere he saw a number of women whom they held in highest honour, women of property, and in some instances a large amount of property, and of the highest intelligence and culture, who were really much more familiar with the questions of the day than half the men were... (applause)"

The two other subscribers were Mrs M. Dungey from Redruth and Mrs Diplock from Falmouth. Through their connections with the Bristol society, they might have been responsible for arranging Miss Blackburn's and Miss Wilkinson's visits. Mrs Dungey, was a member of the Redruth school board and was President of the White Rose Union, a Christian organization, which between 1883 and 1889 held three meetings on women's suffrage and passed resolutions in its support.

Party politics also played a role in the debate. Politically the county was dominated by Liberals, who although always divided over women's suffrage, nationally and locally, contributed a great deal to the debate. In Cornwall two M.P.s were at the forefront of the debate in

Parliament. The most important of these was the Liberal M.P. for Liskeard (1875-1885) and then Bodmin (1885-1900), Leonard Courtney (1832-1918). In Parliament in 1878 he replaced Jacob Bright as leader of the pro-suffrage M.P.s, resigning this position in 1881 when he was appointed Colonial Under-Secretary. He was an executive committee member of the Bristol and West of England Society for Women's Suffrage and later an executive committee member of the Central Committee of the National Society for Women's Suffrage.

Leonard Courtney, later Lord Courtney of Penwith, trained as a barrister and was Professor of Political Economy at University College, London. In 1883 he married Kate Potter (1847-1929), the sister of Beatrice Webb. He was a friend of the President of the NUWSS, Millicent Fawcett, and continued to support women's suffrage until his death. His wife's involvement was more limited. She mainly accompanied her husband to political meetings. She was however persuaded by Millicent Fawcett to join the Women's Suffrage Appeal Committee in 1893. She was also one of the founders of the Women's Liberal Unionist Association in 1888. That year she made her first public speech addressing members at Liskeard Town Hall on October 23rd (Caine 1986, 166). However by the late 1890s her support for this organisation faded, mainly because it supported the Boer War, which both she and her husband opposed. From 1912 until 1915 she was the President of the South Western Federation of the NUWSS.

The second M.P. who played an important role in Parliament was Charles Coneybeare (1853-1919), M.P. for Camborne (1885-1895). He was a former barrister, a radical and Home Ruler, who also campaigned for women's property rights and was joint author of *Conybeare and Andrew's Married Women's Property Acts*. He was a controversial figure as the description of his election illustrates (Deacon 1992, 37-43). His wife, Florence (1872-1916) was a Vice President of the London Society for Women's Suffrage until at least 1914.

Two other Cornish M.P.s supported women's suffrage in Parliament. These were Thomas Owen (1840-1898), Liberal M.P. for

Launceston (1892-1898) and Thomas Bolitho (1835-1915), Liberal Unionist M.P. for St. Ives (1887-1900). Bolitho was a Penzance banker, a magistrate and Deputy Lord Lieutenant for Cornwall. He was related to Mrs Robins Bolitho, who later became one of the first supporters in Penzance of both the WSPU and NUWSS.

Local parliamentary candidates were also interrogated by members of the public, on their views on women's suffrage. This illustrates some of the political divisions. As early as 1875, the M.P. for Liskeard (1869-1876) Mr Horseman stated at a meeting for constituents that (*WSJ* March 1875) "he was against it ...because it was contrary to the design of nature..."an argument often used by the opposition to women's suffrage. Questioning of local candidates gathered momentum after the *1884 Third Parliamentary Reform Act*. For example that year at a meeting in Wadebridge (*WSJ* April 1884), Charles Ross, the Conservative M.P. for St. Ives (1880-1884), stated that he was opposed to women's suffrage. The following year at two election meetings (*WSJ* July, 1885), the sitting Liberal M.P. for West Cornwall, Arthur Pendarves Vivian (1868-1885), addressed crowded meetings at Camborne and Redruth and asserted that he was against women's suffrage (*WSJ* July 1885). He was followed in August by Leonard Courtney who addressed an open air meeting at St. Neot, near Liskeard, where he reasserted his support (*WSJ* September 1885).

Walter Molesworth St. Aubyn, the unsuccessful Conservative candidate for Truro, qualified his support at a meeting in Helston where he had been M.P. (*WSJ* July 1885). He argued that only single women should be given the vote. In 1888 the White Rose Union in Redruth, invited Mr Conybeare to address a meeting. Here he argued that it was for the benefit of all that (*WSJ* November 1888) "women should actively participate in political life." A resolution proposed by Mrs Dungey was then passed.

Finally by the 1880s Liberal Associations were appearing all over England including Cornwall and provided another forum for debating this issue, for example at the first meeting in St Austell in 1885 addressed by Miss Wilkinson, mentioned earlier. This was followed on December 10th, 1901 by a Conference of Delegates from nearly all

34

the Habitations of the Primrose League in Devon, Cornwall, Somerset and Dorset held at Exeter, recommended that (*EWR* January 1902) "they should do all they could to encourage the enfranchisement of women householders."

Meetings were also occasionally held to discuss the issue by local temperance societies. For example the Falmouth Monthly meeting of the Church of England Temperance Society in 1879 (*WSJ* November 1879) voted to support women's suffrage.

Thus although there is no evidence of suffrage activity after the last petition in 1897 until the emergence of the second phase of activity in 1909, the idea of women's suffrage had been widely discussed throughout Cornwall. The lack of discussion during this interim period was in spite of the formation in London of the NUWSS in 1897, which was established in order to form a more cohesive suffrage campaign. It was a national federation of the seventeen largest suffrage societies, including the Bristol and West of England Women's Suffrage Society and heralded the development of a new phase in suffrage activity.

There are many possible reasons for the lack of suffrage activity during this period. Firstly the emergence of other women's political movements, namely the Women's Liberal Federation, the Women's Liberal Association and the inclusion of women in the Primrose League, meant that women had more opportunities to participate on the periphery of political life. This together with the wide acceptance of their participation on local School Boards and Poor Law Boards, might have directed possible suffrage activists' energies towards campaigning .for women to be elected to these rather than concentrating on women's suffrage.

Thirdly the Boer War divided the movement which meant that nationally the movement's activities declined. Some leading activists were preoccupied with the war, for example in 1899 Leonard Courtney, a pacifist, resigned from the Liberal Unionist Party because of its support for the war. In 1900 he addressed a meeting in Liskeard explaining his opposition (Oldfield 1989, 25). The meeting was disrupted and eventually broken up.

35

Fourthly various divisions soon developed within the suffrage movement, resulting in two major organisations, the NUWSS and WSPU. Finally there was the dispiriting lack of progress in Parliament, in spite of the support of many M.P.s. The political parties were still divided with the majority against women's suffrage, either for pragmatic political reasons or because they sincerely felt that women, because of their supposed and alleged emotional and physical frailty, should not be eligible to vote. Added to these, a more local reason must have been a concern with the decline of the Cornish economy and its social consequences which may explain why it took so long for the suffrage debate to re-emerge in Cornwall.

Although the evidence for this first phase of Cornish suffrage activity is rather fragmentary, it does illustrate that the issue was part of the political discourse throughout the county, mainly amongst the liberal middle classes, and occasionally amongst members of the mining and fishing communities. From my reading of *The Women's Suffrage Journal* and *The Englishwoman's Review*, Cornwall was not unusual. What is unusual is that Falmouth set up a suffrage committee so early on in the history of the debate and that there was such a long gap between the first and second phases of the movement.

Words Not Deeds: the women's suffrage campaign, 1909 - 1914

Background

Before the suffrage campaign re-emerged in Cornwall a number of events took place which influenced the national campaign and broadened its support. In 1897 the formation of the National Union of Women's Suffrage Societies (NUWSS) heralded a new phase in the activity of the suffrage movement. The NUWSS was organised more democratically than earlier suffrage organisations in that it was administered by an executive committee that was elected annually by local societies. This committee formulated policy at a yearly council meeting. Local societies funded the organisation by paying an annual subscription.

The aims of the NUWSS were to create a powerful cohesive parliamentary lobby, educate the public, establish branches in all parliamentary constituencies and make women's suffrage a major issue during elections until women's suffrage was granted. It was also a law abiding, constitutional and non-party organisation, although most of its membership came from the Liberal Party. As a result of this programme local societies were gradually formed all over the country, mainly due to the work of nationally paid and voluntary organisers and local supporters.

In 1903 a group of Manchester supporters, led by Emmeline Pankhurst and her daughter Christabel, broke away from the NUWSS because they felt that only women should campaign for women's suffrage. They formed the WSPU, which at first was based in Manchester. In 1905 after Christabel Pankhurst and her friend Annie Kenney heckled Churchill at a public meeting in Manchester, they realised that this more militant behaviour would gain them more support and free publicity. In 1906 the group moved their headquarters to London, appointed a central committee led by the Pankhursts and Frederick and Emmeline Pethick Lawrence. Gradually their activity became more militant and supporters were arrested and imprisoned. This was in spite of a group of activists leaving to form the Women's Freedom League (WFL) in 1907.

In 1909 the first prison hunger strike took place as a demonstration against their treatment as Second Division (criminal) prisoners, rather than as First Division (political) prisoners. In 1910 the WSPU called a truce while the first of the Conciliation Bills was debated. Under pressure from all suffrage groups, the House of Commons set up a committee that was instructed to put forward an acceptable suffrage bill. Although only a minority of women would have benefited, the bill was supported by all political parties and suffrage groups, Asquith, the Prime Minister, managed to either prevent the bill from being debated or have it modified so that at the last Bill's Second Reading in March 1912, it was finally lost.

Meanwhile WSPU support continued to expand until 1912, when Emmeline and Frederick Pethick Lawrence were forced to leave, because of differences they had with Christabel and Emmeline Pankhurst over militant tactics. They formed the Votes for Women Fellowship and in 1914 the United Suffragists. They continued to edit the suffragette journal *Votes for Women* and the WSPU launched a new journal *The Suffragette*.

In the meantime the WSPU adopted more militant tactics such as window smashing and later an arson campaign. In 1913 the Government introduced the infamous '*Cat and Mouse Act*' (the Prisoner's Temporary Discharge for Ill Health Act). This made it more difficult for the WSPU to operate, since suffragettes could be arrested, imprisoned and released at the convenience of the police. The NUWSS throughout this period continued campaigning on a constitutional platform, eventually condemning the WSPU's militancy which they argued was detrimental to the cause.

To begin with in the West Country both the NUWSS and the WSPU focused their activity in Bristol, probably because Bristol was a long established centre for suffrage activity. Gradually both organisations formed societies in the Southwest; first in Devon, then in Wales and finally in 1909 they moved into Cornwall.

In many ways this second but shorter phase of suffrage activity in Cornwall was similar to the first phase since much of the activity was initiated by visiting organisers. Much of their activity mirrored the national movements', although there were differences that made it unique, mainly due to the sparse population in Cornwall. With no large towns, Cornwall was a more difficult area in which to organise events. This was partly overcome by organising specific campaigns such as election and caravan campaigns.

An additional campaign which recruited many supporters, was the use the WSPU in particular made of 'political' tourism, that is, they made use of the fact that by this period Cornwall had become a popular resort venue. Thus suffrage supporters on holiday were encouraged to recruit local members by leafleting and public speaking.

In 1909 both groups began to campaign in Cornwall. This was several years later than in many other areas of Britain, for example, in Oxford which had an NUWSS branch by 1904. Apart from the remoteness of Cornwall, its economic decline and sparse population, all of which had not inhibited the development of the first phase, there seems to be no reason for this relatively late emergence.

By 1910 Cornish supporters were participating in national demonstrations, such as the Coronation March in 1911, a march organised by the NUWSS and WSPU to put pressure on the new King, George V and Parliament. Most importantly they formed local societies. At first the membership of both groups overlapped, as it did elsewhere, but by 1912 they were in competition with each other and by the end of 1913 the NUWSS dominated Cornish activity. This was partly due to the failure of the Conciliation Bills in 1912, and from 1913 the increasing use of more non-conventional militant methods by the WSPU. It was also due to the larger number of local societies established by the NUWSS that gave them a stronger local foothold. This was in line with the national pattern, since the NUWSS relied much more on local societies to contribute to policy-making than the highly centralised WSPU. The NUWSS was also helped by regional federations. In 1911 the South Western Federation was established in Devon and Cornwall. This gave valuable support to NUWSS members

39

and societies, as well linking them formally to other parts of the country.

In the same way in which the earlier campaigns remained unaffected by the divisions within the movement, there is little evidence that these affected local Cornish groups. In other parts of England other suffrage societies such as the WFL had established groups. Some members of these groups, particularly the WFL and the Free Church League for Women's Suffrage, occasionally addressed meetings in Cornwall. Similarly no one local society dominated the whole county in the way in which both the Oxford WSPU and NUWSS dominated Oxfordshire or the Cambridge societies dominated Cambridgeshire.

Formal opposition to the suffrage movement was becoming well established by 1908, and by 1912 the National League for Opposing Women's Suffrage (NLOWS) had established branches all over the country. However there is no trace of any formal opposition in Cornwall, in spite of earlier plans in 1912 until the summer of 1914 when NLOWS planned to establish branches in the county (*Anti-Suffrage Review* September 1912 and August 1914). This objective coincided with the advent of the First World War and meant that these plans were not realised.

The lack of organised opposition is surprising since the WSPU in particular campaigned intensively in Cornwall. It was their activities that elsewhere caused anti-suffragists to establish branches. The reason for this lack of opposition was possibly determined by the WSPU not resorting to more outright militancy in Cornwall. Occasionally there was informal local opposition although this was mainly towards the NUWSS rather than the WSPU, possibly because to the general public these two organisations were indistinguishable.

It is against this background that I will analyse this second phase of suffrage activity, concentrating on their campaigning techniques. These include activity such as public meetings, canvassing and specific campaigns as well as an examination of their membership. The role played by the host of 'visitors' and the networks which were established between the different local societies, their members and the national organisations. All of this is well documented in the national suffrage journals and to a lesser extent in local newspapers.

Militancy? the WSPU campaign

In 1908 the WSPU set up a West of England Society in Bristol. Gradually its campaign extended westwards to include Plymouth and Torbay. It was coordinated by Annie Kenney who had formed the Bristol WSPU in 1907. Annie (1879-1953) was a former Oldham mill worker, who in 1906 left her home to help organise the WSPU campaign in London, at a salary of £2 a week. She was a close friend of Christabel Pankhurst's and from various accounts by other suffragettes was equally charismatic. In May 1908 she formulated her plans for a West of England campaign. She remained organiser until 1911 and travelled all over the region, including Cornwall. She usually travelled with another WSPU worker and together they would contact known local supporters, leaflet, chalk pavements to advertise local meetings, speak at open air meetings and convene more formal public meetings. Their aim was to set up a local committee in as many local towns as possible. Once this was achieved they would return later to ensure that the committee continued its activities.

In March 1909 she and Mary Howey visited Penzance, the most southwesterly town in Cornwall. This was the beginning of a spectacularly intensive campaign that continued throughout most of that year. The object of this was to secure a firm foothold in Cornwall.

Although Mary Howey and Mary Phillips, two other WSPU organizers together with Mary Blathwayt, had organised meetings in November 1908 in Saltash, (Blathwayt 1908) the campaign in Cornwall was not launched officially until March 1909. On March 8th Annie Kenney travelled to Penzance and stayed with Mary Howey in Newlyn. The campaign was then inaugurated by a large public meeting on March 12th, addressed by Annie Kenney and Mary Howey and presided over by a local supporter, Miss Booth Scott (*VW* March 12th, 1909). At the meeting, attended by 600 people, Annie Kenney made an appeal for £100 to fund a Cornish organiser (*VW* March 19th, 1908). The next day a drawing room meeting was held and participants formed the first Cornish WSPU committee. Annie Kenney then left, leaving the local committee, led by their new secretary, Mrs Powell, to organise a series of open air meetings in Penzance and neighbouring villages, with local members selling *Votes for Women*.

In May the committee accepted the unpaid services of a national organiser, Dorothy Pethick. Together with local members, she, Annie Kenney and Mary Blathwayt, called another large public meeting in Penzance on June 2nd (*VW* June 11th, 1909). This was addressed by Dorothy's sister, Emmeline Pethick Lawrence and Lady Constance Lytton and chaired by Annie Kenney. Lady Constance Lytton spoke about her conversion to militancy earlier that year and her arrest during a deputation to the Prime Minister and subsequent imprisonment in Holloway. Apart from speeches, the programme included music and literature was sold and money collected. The hall itself was festooned with purple, green and white flowers, the WSPU colours. During the meeting an unforeseen event took place which involved Mr Vaughan T Paul, a photographer, whilst standing under the balcony in the hall (*St. Ives Weekly Summary* June 12th, 1909):

`... he fired the flashlight powder, which was largely composed of magnesium, and as the result of the close proximity of the balcony, the flash was thrown into his face. His moustache, eyebrows, and eyelashes were burnt off, and his face scorched.'

In spite of this unfortunate occurrence the meeting was a great success since as one working man was quoted (*VW* June 11th, 1909) "all the town is talking of it."

Mary Blathwayt's diaries record the events daily and illustrate the way in which this part of the campaign was organised, as well as the appeal that Cornwall had for activists to indulge in a certain amount of relaxation. On May 28th, she and Annie travelled by train from Bristol to Penzance.

'We were met by one member at Penzance station. We drove a cab here (at a Mrs Shannon's house, 'Treere', in Sennen), where Annie and I are staying.'

On the following day she wrote:

'This morning Annie and I sat on the rocks at the Landsend [sic] and watched some gulls with young ones. This afternoon we walked to the Whitesands, and had tea at the little house by the Landsend.'

For the next two days they walked, sat amongst the rocks and wrote letters. On the 2nd they moved to Mrs Moir's house, 'Lynwood Paul', Mousehole. Mrs Moir was a member of the Penzance branch of the WSPU. Mary's diary continues:

'This morning Annie and I drove over to Penzance with Mrs Moir and Miss M. Duncan and the little girl, Mrs Moir's daughter. We went to St. John's Hall and helped arrange flowers for the meeting. The Lord Mayor arrived with a band and crowds of people as we came out and they insisted upon taking down our Votes for Women banner, as it was mixed up with the decorations for the Lord Mayor of London. I went with Mrs Howey to 18 Cornwall Terrace and wrote letters in the morning. Then Mrs and Mary Howey, Dorothy Pethick and I had lunch with Mrs Bache, 3, St Mary's Place. I also had tea there. Went to Mrs Powell's (house) Roseleigh Alverton and changed into my white dress for the meeting at 8 p.m.. Annie was in the chair, Mrs P Lawrence and Lady Constance Lytton spoke. I sold literature, 2/4 worth, and collected 8/4 1/2 in a tin at one of the doors afterwards. A photograph was taken of the speakers for the *Daily Mirror*, but the photographer had his face badly burned by flash lights and had to be taken off to a doctor. We drove back to Mousehole again after the meeting and had to come the long way round as the road was up.'

The following day was spent in Penzance and Mousehole:

'It has been raining today. This morning I wrote a letter. Annie went over to Penzance for a members meeting and to see Mrs Pethick Lawrence and Lady Constance Lytton off. Dorothy Pethick came back with Annie for the afternoon. Some people came to tea. Mary Duncan, Annie and I walked part of the way back to Penzance with Dorothy Pethick.'

After the public meeting, as Mary Blathwayt and *Votes for Women* describe, Dorothy Pethick, Annie Kenney and the committee mapped out an immediate and massive programme of meetings throughout much of the county (see Table 2). The intention was for speakers to visit each place in the neighbourhood weekly and to daily hold two meetings. The speakers were mainly drawn from local supporters who were helped by Dorothy Pethick, Mrs Howey and Dorothy Bowker.

Local speakers included Mrs Moir who had not only looked after Annie Kenney and Mary Blathwayt, but also paid for the publicity for the first meeting in Penzance; Mary Duncan, and Mrs Powell and her daughter, Blanche, who later 'came out' as a fervent WSPU member in 1911 (*VW* August 4, 1911). Some members also volunteered to join the WSPU deputation to the Prime Minister, on June 29th.

Table 2. Meetings organised June 1909.
Source: *Votes for Women* June 1909

Date and Time		Place	Speakers
June 11	3.30	Camborne	Mrs Howey, Miss Powell
	7.30	Redruth	Miss Howey, Mrs Bowker
June 12	3.30	Falmouth	Miss Scott, Miss Pethick
June 14	8.00	St. Ives	Miss Scott, Mrs Howey, Miss Bertram
June 16	?	Newlyn	?
June 17	?	Penzance	Miss Scott
June 18	7.00	Redruth	Miss Howey, Miss Bowker
	?	Helston	?
June 19	3.00	Falmouth	Miss Howey, Miss Bowker, Miss Pethick
June 21	7.30	St. Ives	Miss Pethick, Miss Scott, Miss Duncan, Mrs Moir
June 22	3.00	Truro	Miss Pethick
	3.00	Falmouth	Miss Howey, Miss Bowker
June 23	8.00	Falmouth	Miss Bowker, Miss Pethick
June 24	3.30	Penzance	Miss Scott, Mrs Powell, Miss Nance
	7.30	Penzance	Miss Pethick, Miss Howey
June 29	3.00	Falmouth	?

N.B. During this period there were also meetings at Newlyn, Marazion, Mousehole, Camborne and Redruth.

Dorothy Bowker came down to Cornwall for the sole purpose of addressing meetings to encourage local members to join the deputation. In fact she, like many other members of this deputation, was arrested together with one Cornish woman, Annie Williams, another national organiser.

The work rapidly became too much for Dorothy Pethick and after a request to London, Miss Winifred Jones, a Chesterfield suffragette, came down to help her. Dorothy Pethick's work was curtailed as she was arrested during the deputation in London and then imprisoned for a short period. She was replaced by another WSPU organizer, Mary Phillips who continued her programme until she too was arrested in Exeter at a demonstration against a visiting government Minister. She together, with a later speaker, Elsie Howey, went on hunger strike in Exeter gaol. Mary was released on medical grounds after three days (*VW* August 6th and 13th, 1909).

In spite of these difficulties the meetings continued with almost as much intensity throughout much of the next month. Between July 2nd and 23rd meetings were held in Penzance, Falmouth, St. Ives, Camborne, Redruth and Hayle. This was followed by more campaigning in August and September, partly organised by Mary Phillips, who returned to Cornwall after her short imprisonment, and partly by visitors who organised the first holiday campaign (see later). Throughout this period *Votes for Women* were sold and funds continued to be raised for an organiser. The latter campaign was helped in September by the artist Malcolm Smith who donated a miniature of Christabel Pankhurst (*VW* September 13th, 1909). This was sold to the highest bidder at the next large public meeting in the autumn. As soon as the holiday campaign ended, an autumn campaign was launched, focusing on two public meetings in Launceston and Truro on October 21st and 22nd respectively (*VW* October 29th, 1909). These were addressed again by Mrs Pethick Lawrence and Annie Kenney.

The WSPU then expanded its activities by holding open air and drawing room meetings for teachers, shop assistants and nurses, as well as carrying out door-to-door canvassing in these two towns. At the end of October, Mary Phillips left Cornwall to work in the North of England. She was replaced by a Welsh suffragette, Miss Edith Williams, who centred her activities in her house at 'Glenafan' in the small village of Devoran, between Falmouth and Truro, where she lived until 1914. The final meeting in 1909, was an 'At Home' held in Truro (*VW* November 19th, 1909) addressed by Miss Elsie Howey, Mary Howey's younger sister.

Thus, all during this first year of WSPU campaigning, a series of national organisers, mainly based at Tregenna House in Penzance, and helped by periodic visits from Annie Kenney, were in charge. Only during the holiday campaign was a second centre used by Mary Phillips. This was 9, The Parade, Truro.

All of the early organisers worked closely together not only in Cornwall but throughout the West of England. All of them had been arrested at a demonstration that year. They were also unmarried and relatively young women, as were the majority of WSPU organisers. This is not surprising since they were all expected to devote their lives to the cause, were expected to travel a great deal and spend all their energy co-ordinating public events.

The first organiser, Dorothy Pethick (1881-1970) was the younger sister of Emmeline Pethick Lawrence, the Treasurer of the WSPU. From 1908 she began to address public meetings and became a national WSPU travelling organiser. The Pethicks were a large West Country Quaker family, originally from Cornwall. Like her elder sister Emmeline, she was interested in social issues and before joining the WSPU had trained at a university settlement and worked as a superintendent of a girls' club in Nottingham. In 1909 she was arrested twice, imprisoned once, and went on hunger strike and was force-fed. She then resumed work as a travelling organiser, working in Leicester, Reading and Oxford. In 1914 Dorothy joined the Women's Auxiliary Service (Women's Police).

She was followed by Mary Howey, who was helped by her mother. This family probably contributed more than any other to the Cornish suffragette campaign. Mary and her sister Elsie Howey (1884-1963) were the daughters of Thomas (the Rector of Finningley, Nottinghamshire) and his wife, Gertrude. After the Reverend Howey's death, the family moved to Worcestershire. Mrs Howey was a WSPU supporter, not only speaking in Cornwall, but contributing funds to other societies elsewhere in the country. Mary was a vegetarian, like many suffragettes. She probably was a painter of some note, since in 1912 she is recorded by Mary Blathwayt as spending time in Bath, at the home of the President of the Anti-suffragists, where she painted her dogs.

Elsie Howey (1884-1963) attended St. Andrew's University from 1902 to 1904 and then went to Germany. She joined the WSPU in 1908. She was frequently arrested from 1908 onwards and served some of the longest sentences given out to suffragette prisoners. In 1909 she worked as an unpaid organiser in Devon, although this was interspersed with imprisonment. Her life continued in this vein until 1914. She was well known not only for her spectacular demonstrations but also for dressing up as Joan of Arc, first riding at the head of a welcoming committee, on Emmeline Pethick Lawrence's release from Holloway in April 1909 and then in 1913 at Emily Wilding Davison's funeral, accompanying her coffin. Her intention was to give up her life for the cause. In effect she did this, or at least her voice was sacrificed, ruined by the cumulative effects of force feeding.

Mary Phillips (1880-1969) like Dorothy Pethick had connections with Cornwall. She was the daughter of W. Fleming Phillips, a surgeon, and his wife, Elizabeth Louise, both WSPU supporters. Originally they had lived in St. Mary Bourne in Hampshire, where Mary was born, then moved to Glasgow and later Falmouth. From 1908 onwards she worked as a paid organiser and like Elsie Howey, although less flamboyant, was frequently arrested and imprisoned. She returned to Cornwall at the end of 1912 when her mother died after some years of ill-health. After Cornwall she went to work in the North of England and returned to the south-west, to Plymouth in 1913. Later that year she worked as an organiser for Sylvia Pankhurst's breakaway group, the East London Federation of the Suffragettes, under a pseudonym, 'Mary Patterson'. She was responsible for the name of its journal, *The Worker's Dreadnought*. She continued to work and participate in political causes throughout her life. In 1914 she joined and worked for the United Suffragists. She later worked for the

Women's International League and the Save the Children Fund. In 1928 she worked as editor of a daily news service for the brewing trade, retiring in 1955. She was a socialist, a Fabian and a member of the Six Point Group.

The final member of this group of organisers was Edith Williams, a Welsh suffragette who was born in Llanelly, on the Welsh borders. Apart from this, no more details of her life have been found.

After this period of intensive campaigning, brought together by this group of energetic women, there was a short lull in activity during which the NUWSS began to establish itself in East Cornwall, an area untouched by the WSPU. In May 1910, the two joint secretaries, Mrs Powell and Miss Edith Williams working for the newly named Cornwall society (formerly Penzance), organised another intensive campaign which included the return visit of Elsie Howey. She addressed a meeting in Penzance on a favourite WSPU topic, "Women and the sweated industries and why this demonstrated the need to give women the vote" (*VW* May 13th, 1910). After this meeting Cornish members like suffragettes elsewhere, postponed meetings to mark the King's death. Some also joined a large demonstration jointly promoted by the WSPU and NUWSS in London, the Coronation March. In October after the second holiday campaign, public meetings were resumed, this time addressed by a national speaker, Miss Maria Brackenbury who visited Devoran, Truro and Falmouth. (*VW* October 14th, 1910). She like many other visitors stayed at 'Glenafon'. Maria Brackenbury (1866-1950) was a landscape painter, newspaper columnist and cartoonist, based in London. Like the other visiting speakers she had been arrested many times.

In October 1910 WSPU supporters were making preparations for a visit by Mrs Pankhurst who was to address a meeting on October 29th. This unfortunately had to be postponed the day before (*VW* November 11th, 1910). Finally after an election campaign in Falmouth, a new branch was established there (*VW* December 23rd, 1910).

48

Table 3. WSPU Branches in Cornwall, 1909 - 1914.
Source: *Votes for Women* (incomplete)

Penzance: March 1909, referred to as Cornwall from April 1910

President:	1909-1910	Mrs Powell
Hon. Secretary:	1910-1911	Miss Edith Williams
		Mrs Powell
	1911-1914	Miss Edith Williams
Organiser:	1909	Miss Dorothy Pethick
		Miss Mary Howey
		Miss Mary Phillips
	1909-1910	Miss Edith Williams

Falmouth: December 1910, reformed as Falmouth and Penryn in October 1911

Hon. Secretary:	1910-1911	Miss Ross
	1911-1912	Mrs Jane Pascoe)
		Mrs English)
	1912-1914	Mrs Jane Pascoe
Hon. Treasurer:	1911-1912	Miss Richards
	1912	Mrs K. Pascoe
Press Secretary:	1912	Mrs F. Corbett
Organiser:	1911-1912	Mrs F. Corbett

Newquay: March 1913 - June 1914

| Hon. Secretary: | 1913-1914 | Miss A. Clemes |

Between 1911 and 1912 campaigning was organised from Falmouth and Devoran. In Falmouth a new organiser, Mrs Corbett and the local secretary, Miss Ross lived at 'The Bungalow'. Mrs Catherine Isabel Ida Corbett (nee Vans Agnew) was rather different from the other WSPU workers in Cornwall. Not only was she married but also came from a landowning family rather than from a middle class one. She was the daughter of George Vans Agnew, a civil servant in India, the descendant of an old Scots land-owning family. She married Frank

Corbett, a yachtsman, a commodore of the Royal Norfolk and Suffolk Yacht Club, part owner of Daneshill in Sussex and brother of a Liberal M.P.. Like Dorothy Bowker, she was drawn into the WSPU by witnessing the 'dignity and courage' of Emmeline Pankhurst when she was arrested in 1908 (*VW* July 2nd, 1907). Like the other WSPU organisers she was arrested, first in 1909 for participating in a deputation to the Prime Minister on February 26th, and then later on that year at a demonstration in Dundee.

Meetings in 1911 included another addressed by Mrs Pethick Lawrence, this time accompanied by the Australian suffragette, Miss Vida Goldstein (*VW* April 28th, 1911). The latter returned to Cornwall with Annie Kenney to address a meeting in Newquay in July (*VW* July 21st, 1911). Vida Goldstein (1869-1949) was a leading Australian suffrage campaigner, the first woman to stand, albeit unsuccessfully, for the Australian Parliament in 1903. In 1911 she paid her first visit to England as a guest of the WSPU and returned again in 1913.

In February 1911 Mrs Corbett, in line with national WSPU policy, put forward a petition to a member of the Conciliation Committee, the Liberal Unionist M.P. for Falmouth, Mr Goldman, in order to persuade him to support the Conciliation Bill. The petition was signed by 170 ratepayers including the Liberal Mayor of Penryn and the Conservative Mayor of Falmouth. Later Mrs Corbett interviewed Mr Hay Morgan, Liberal M.P. for Truro, who promised to support the Bill. Both Falmouth and Truro Town Councils gave their support to the Bill in line with Councils across the country.

By the summer of 1911 the Falmouth branch was suffering from competition from a large NUWSS branch. As a result, in October, it was re-launched as the Falmouth and Penryn branch. Two new secretaries were elected, Mrs Pascoe and Mrs English. Mrs Corbett remained as organiser. The branch held regular fortnightly meetings, mainly on the Conciliation Bill, including two in the Town Hall (*VW* November 3rd, 1911) addressed by Miss Isabel Seymour, a national worker and friend of Mrs Pethick Lawrence.

At the beginning of 1912 Mrs Pethick Lawrence returned a third time to Cornwall, this time accompanied by a friend, Mrs Mabel Tuke, the WSPU 's Secretary from 1907 until 1912. They stayed in Falmouth and members arranged a special 'At Home' for them at the Royal Hotel (*VW* January 5th, 1912). However, that year the Cornish WSPU faced organisational problems. Firstly in March, Mrs Pascoe was arrested and imprisoned for a month in Holloway, for participating in the WSPU window smashing campaign (*VW,* March 8th, 1912).

'The Constable giving evidence said that he saw the defendant throw three stones at the window of the Board of Education building, breaking two panes of glass of 10 s value. ... He went up to her and asked her why she did it, and she replied "Justice to Women." She was then arrested.'

On her return, on May 30th, she took over as treasurer and sole secretary of the Falmouth and Penryn branch.

Secondly, Mrs Corbett was bedevilled with 'private' problems and left Cornwall in September (*VW* September 13th, 1912). Members managed in spite of this to continue selling *Votes for Women* and hold public meetings. In July they also participated in a new national campaign against the force feeding of suffragette prisoners. They successfully petitioned local doctors to voice their objections to this (*VW,* July 19th, 1912).

Gradually the Cornish campaign moved its centre to Truro, where from the end of 1912 until 1914 monthly meetings were held (see Table 4). What was noticeable about these meetings is that they were addressed by a mixture of local and national speakers, including Hatty Baker, a leading member of the Free Church League for Women's Suffrage. They were also no longer reliant on national organisers, although Mary Phillips (who was based in Plymouth) visited periodically. The reason for her initial visit however was a personal one. Her mother died, after months of ill health, at the beginning of December, having refused to contact her daughter since she felt that the WSPU needed her services more (*SU*, December 13th, 1912).

Table 4. Monthly meetings in Truro 1912 - 1914.
Source: *The Suffragette (SU)* (incomplete)

Date	Speaker	Topic
1912		
December 7	Mrs Perks, Mrs Tremayne, Mrs Pascoe	Future plans.
1913		
February 1	Mrs Perks, Miss E. Williams	Discussion on new developments
March 1	Mary Phillips	
April	Rev. H. Baker	The White Slave trade
June	Miss Simmons	Teachers & Suffrage
	Mrs Perks	Prison experience
July	?	?
November 8	Miss Clarence	Forcible feeding
December 5	Mrs Tremayne, Mrs Perks	Defence of militancy
	Miss E. Williams	Sweated labour
1914		
February /	Miss Simmons	'The Great Scourge'
April 4	Rev. H. Baker	?
May 2	?	

Meetings were also held outside Truro, for example, a successful open air meeting in Falmouth on March 5th, was addressed by Joan Dugdale and Mary Phillips (*SU*, March 7th, 1913). Joan Dugdale, was a short story writer who came from a leading suffrage family. She joined the WSPU in 1907, was later the organising secretary of the Actresses' Franchise League and was arrested several times. An even more successful meeting was the inaugural one at Newquay (*SU*, April 11th, 1913), addressed by the redoubtable Mrs Drummond, a leading and popular WSPU organiser and speaker. Here the one act of militancy in Cornwall took place on June 8th, 1914 when the tennis courts were attacked causing some damage (Metcalfe, 1917). Shortly after this Newquay WSPU became an NUWSS society.

In the autumn a demonstration was organised by Mrs Tremayne, a former member of the Conservative and Unionist Party, outside a Primrose League Meeting in Truro (*SU*, September 5th, 1913). In the following months, local and national activity focused again on forcible feeding. This time WSPU supporters distributed leaflets outside a Liberal meeting in Truro, addressed a meeting in Redruth,and made an appeal to Cornish clergyman.

In the early months of 1914 Mrs Pascoe was ill and her role as secretary was taken over by two Penzance activists, Mrs Powell and her daughter. Although suffragette activity continued that year it was overshadowed by NUWSS activity. The one exception was in Truro where members continued their monthly meetings. By the outbreak of World War I there was no campaigning in Cornwall by local members, although plans (*SU*, August 7th, 1914) were in place for a holiday campaign. These never came to fruition.

This decline in activity may have been because members became disillusioned with the WSPU's growing militancy, especially the arson attacks and the pillar box campaign. Unlike other areas, in Cornwall, members did not take part in militant activities and such restraint was indicative of their attitudes. Cornish members may also have been sympathetic towards the stand taken by the Pethick Lawrences in 1912, against increasing militancy. Emmeline was a very popular figure in Cornwall since she emphasised her family links with Cornwall.

Apart from the visiting organisers and speakers already mentioned, there were other 'visitors' who helped to set up activities during the summer holidays. From 1909 until 1914, the WSPU had a policy, publicised in *Votes for Women* and their *Annual Report*, of urging members to initiate or participate in local campaigns whilst on holiday. Prior to this, individual members had held 'impromptu' meetings whilst on holiday. Cornwall was a popular holiday destination. It, together with Torquay, was referred to by *The Suffragette* (August 12th, 1913) as 'the English Riviera campaign'. It was, therefore, not surprising that summer holiday campaigns took place annually in Cornwall. Members were instructed that, if on holiday, they should work either with an existing branch or with existing members in order to recruit new supporters and if possible start a branch where none existed.

The first Cornish campaign began on August 6th, 1909 in St. Ives where three suffragettes, Mary Bell, Miss Brown and Miss Mansell-Jones stayed at York House that belonged to Miss Wade, a Cornish supporter (*VW* August 13th, 1909). Eventually their campaigning spread across Cornwall to encompass the north coast, closing in mid September. During this campaign members sold *Votes for Women*, recruited new members, held open-air meetings and chalked pavements. At least nine women were involved, sometimes working with Mary Phillips. For example (*VW*, August 13th, 1909)

"... a decorated brake will run from Penzance early in the afternoon to Sennen, where a meeting will be held, after which the flag will be erected on the furthest accessible westerly part of England and left flying there."

Apparently this was so successful that a similar event took place in 1913, just after the NUWSS pilgrimage in June, which started at Land's End (*SU*, September 5th, 1913)

'One of the most interesting touches of the holiday campaign was the planting of the purple, white and green flag on the last crag of England. That rugged rock so well known all the world over, was the resting place for a copy of the *Suffragette*... From all accounts the walk from Falmouth to Land's End attracted much attention and the words most often heard were "Suffragettes everywhere".'

After the first holiday campaign, campaigns were shorter and relied on fewer visitors. Apart from targeting Penzance, Truro and Falmouth they kept mainly to the north coast. These campaigners used various methods of campaigning, for example, in 1910 Miss Constance I. Craig, known locally as "the Suffragette", spent her time riding a bicycle to isolated villages and placed *Votes for Women* in bus shelters and libraries (*VW* September 23rd, 1910).

In 1912 a report in *Votes for Women* (September 13th) described the campaign in detail. It reported on,

'a new speaker's nervousness overcome, of the indignation of the inhabitants, who said the town must not be judged by the rude behaviour of a few "imported" "young gents", of orderly and attentive meetings, excellent sales of the paper, visits on market days to neighbouring towns, where awe-struck children who had never before seen a real live lady chalking the pavements whispered "them must be suffragettes", of requests to hold evening meetings when the women could come too, of many questions asked and answered, and a collection taken from the steps outside the market place, of a sailing boat flying the colours from the masthead and peak ("she was the fastest craft in the bay") and of the mobbing of the suffragettes at one place by boys, whilst a number of schoolgirls formed themselves into a bodyguard and conducted the suffragettes in triumph to their lunch place. "Cornish people," says this worker, "are descended from a warlike race, and their ancestors have fought desperately for existence and liberty, and they seemed to understand the spirit in which we are fighting."'

In 1913, the enterprising Mrs Oliver (*SU*, August 22nd, 1913)

'...has taken a tent on the beach, and, with a WSPU flag flying from the top and a copy of the *Suffragette* pinned on the outside, she and her little daughter sell the paper to passers-by. "No one passes without a word of some sort," she writes, "a laugh, or a word of sympathy. We shall be here for two or three weeks longer, and I am looking for someone who will take our tent, etc, and keep the flag flying when we leave".'

Although as this account of WSPU activities has demonstrated, the role played by national visitors was important, local women also played a key part in the campaign. They are however much more elusive. As I mentioned earlier, a number became members of the NUWSS. They include Mrs Bolitho and Miss Bache, both from Penzance, and Miss Clemes from Newquay. More details of two other local supporters, Miss Annie Williams and Mrs Tremayne, exist.

Annie Williams (c 1860-1943) was a Cornishwoman, a former headmistress and teacher, who in 1908 gave up her job to work for the WSPU as a paid organiser in Bristol. In September she returned to her post in Cornwall, but kept in touch with Annie Kenney. The following year she resumed her job with the WSPU, this time as a travelling organiser. Like other WSPU workers she was arrested, in her case three times. Firstly, on June 29th, 1909, then on August Bank Holiday that year, when she and three others were brutally mobbed at Canford Park, Dorset, and finally in June 1910. She periodically returned to Cornwall on holiday, and addressed meetings. She stayed with Edith Williams, who as far as I can ascertain was not related. In 1914 she visited the exiled Christabel Pankhurst in Paris.

There are fewer details concerning Mrs Tremayne. She lived in Carclew, not far from Falmouth and was married to Captain William Tremayne, a former Captain of the 4th Dragoon Guards. He was closely related to the Tremayne family, the owners of Heligan. She was a member of the Conservative Party and left it to join the WSPU. Although she appears not to have had an official position, she organised many events and frequently addressed public meetings.

The reason why details concerning local supporters are scarce is because the WSPU, unlike the NUWSS, did not have a policy of keeping membership lists. Although it published subscription lists many of the subscribers are anonymous. However, for the WSPU to keep up the momentum in Cornwall, it would have needed a substantial number of activists to help the organisers and local committees. There was also a great deal of interest in its activities since its public meetings were well attended and well recorded by both the local press and suffrage journals.

In contrast the majority of 'visitors' were all well known, often controversial, contemporary figures. The two most important were Annie Kenney (described previously) and Emmeline Pethick Lawrence (1867-1954). Emmeline was important because she was the Treasurer of the WSPU and together with her husband edited and financed *Votes for Women*, which kept local supporters in touch with national policy, progress in Parliament and with other local groups. In Cornwall

56

Emmeline was extremely popular since she emphasised her Cornish connections and was passionately committed to social democratic ideals. Her family originated in Cornwall where her grandfather's family had farmed and owned land in Lanoy. Once he had established his business in Bristol, he built a large house there. Emmeline's family lived in Weston-super-Mare. After a Quaker upbringing, she left home to work for the West London Mission. Here she worked among poor women in the London slums. Together with Mary Neal she founded the Esperance Girls' Club. This pioneering enterprise provided a co-operative workshop, a residential hostel and a holiday home. In 1899 she met her future husband Frederick Lawrence who was then working in the East End Settlement. They were married in 1901.

Frederick's grandfather also originally came from Cornwall. He was a carpenter from St. Agnes, who when he was 19 years old walked to Plymouth. Eventually he become a master builder and owned a large building firm. One of Frederick's uncles, Sir Edwin Durning was Liberal Unionist M.P. for Truro (1895-1906). In 1901 Frederick, a Cambridge graduate, bought a newspaper *The Echo* which he then edited. This had been founded by another Cornishman, John Passmore Edwards.

Apart from these Cornish connections Emmeline spent her summer holidays in St. Ives in the 1890s. Here she made friends with Edith Ellis, the wife of Havelock Ellis, the sexologist. Edith was a writer, businesswoman and had a farm on the moor, above Carbis Bay. Emmeline continued to visit her after she was married. Thus she was familiar with Cornwall. The Pethick Lawrences continued to actively participate in politics during and after the First World War, which is another story.

The suffragette 'visitors' enabled the Cornish WSPU supporters and activists to be part of the mainstream of WSPU activity. They provided them with an important network which prevented the area from becoming isolated, even though they did not actively participate in the later more militant campaigns. The WSPU maintained these networks throughout the country in this way, and managed to ensure their support, in spite of being a highly centralised, undemocratic organisation, dominated by the Pankhursts. Interestingly nearly all the visitors were friends of Annie Kenney or Emmeline Pethick Lawrence and had participated in demonstrations and been imprisoned. These factors must have attracted support and added glamour to a campaign which otherwise would have been fairly prosaic.

The National Union of Women's Suffrage Societies (NUWSS)

In 1909 after the NUWSS had formed a Federation in the West of England, members concentrated on establishing societies in Exeter and Plymouth and then turned their attention to Cornwall. The first society was established in November 1909 (officially affiliated to the NUWSS in February 1910), in the small town of Liskeard, well away from WSPU activity (*CC*, February 24th, 1910). Sometime in 1911 the South Western Federation was established. It was partly as a result of their work that societies were formed in the majority of Cornish towns (see Table 5). Apart from Liskeard, which experienced difficulties in 1913, all survived until at least 1917.

Table 5. NUWSS local executive committees, 1910-1915.
Source: *Common Cause* (incomplete)

Liskeard: February 1910, renamed East Cornwall in 1911.

President:	1910-	Mrs George Hermon
Hon.Secretary:	1910-1913	Miss Jessie Williams
	1913	Miss Mattieson M.A.
		(pro tem)

Penzance: March 1911, re-organized May 1912.

President:	1914-1915	Miss Caroline Borlase
Hon.Secretary:	1911-1912	Mrs Hodgson Pratt & Mrs Bache
	1912-1913	Mrs Glave Saunders
	1913-1915	Mrs Margaret Cornish
Hon. Treasurer:	1911-1915	Mrs Bache

Falmouth: March 1910.

President:	1913-1915	Miss Frances Sterling
Hon. Secretary:	1911-1912	Miss Naomi Bassett Fox & Miss Cicely Broad

Hon. Sec. cont.	1912-1914	Miss Naomi Bassett Fox
	1914-1915	Miss Alston
Hon. Treasurer:	1911-1915	Mrs Isabel Stephens

Wadebridge: May 1912.

President:	1912-1915	Mrs Emily Macmillan
Hon. Secretary:	1912-1915	Miss Helen Symons
Hon. Treasurer:	1914-1915	Mrs Jas Collins

Truro: November 1912.

President:	1914-1915	Mrs Hamilton
Hon. Secretary:	1913-1915	Miss M.J. Robinson
Hon. Treasurer:	1914-1915	Miss M.J. Robinson

St. Ives: November 1912

President:	1914-1915	Mrs Augusta Lindner
Hon. Secretary:	1912-1915	Mrs F Crichton Matthew
Hon.Treasurer:	1914-1915	Mrs Skinner

Saltash and District: April, 1913.

Hon Secretary.	1913-1914	Mrs Margery Jones
	1914-1915	Mrs Waller
Hon. Treasurer:	1914-1915	Mrs Keast

Launceston: October 1913.

| Hon. Secretary: | 1913-1915 | Miss Alice Wevill |
| Hon. Treasurer: | 1914-1915 | Miss Kelly |

Newquay: July 1914.

President:	1914-1915	Rev. W. Huntley Neales
Hon. Secretary:	1914-1915	Miss A. Clemes
Hon.Treasurer:	1914-1915	Mrs Crosby-Smith

According to reports in *Common Cause* the most active although not the largest, was the Falmouth group that by 1912 had 80, and by 1914 had 118 members. This is not surprising, given its earlier history, since it was dominated by the same Quaker families. The largest group, in spite of competition from the WSPU, was in Truro that in 1914 had 137 members. The other societies by 1914 had between 50 and 80 members. The membership, because of the relative smallness of the towns was much lower than in Devon, where, for example, the largest society was Exeter that in 1914 had 263 members.

Rather like the WSPU, the majority of these societies were established by national organisers who ensured that local committees were elected. These committees then became responsible for running their own activities. Thus, although visiting suffrage workers played an important role in setting up the Cornish societies, they did not continue to dominate activity in quite the same way as the WSPU organisers did. They could rely on the locally elected committees to sustain the campaign and if necessary call on the support of the South Western Federation and its paid and voluntary organisers to help them do this. The NUWSS campaign was dominated by a combination of public meetings, open air and indoor; the 1910 Election campaign; the 1911 holiday campaign; the 1913 Pilgrimage, one route starting at Land's End and traversing the county; and in 1914 a caravan campaign.

When the first NUWSS meeting was held in Liskeard, addressed by Helen Fraser, it was obviously a popular move since a hundred members immediately joined (CC, February 24th, 1910). This meant that there must have been earlier if dormant support. It also meant that Helen Fraser was an important catalyst. She was, in fact, a frequent visitor to Cornwall and indeed to the whole of the West and South of England. In some ways she was the most important NUWSS organiser to visit Cornwall, since not only did she help launch the Liskeard Society but later toured the county and was the main speaker on the Cornish section of the Pilgrimage.

In Helen's autobiography (Moyes, 1971) she described how she became involved in the suffrage movement. She came from a large Scottish family. Her father, James Fraser, was a tailor's cutter who worked in Edinburgh and later established a wholesale clothing firm. He was President of the National Federation of Foremen and a member of Glasgow City Council. After finishing her education she set up a studio in Glasgow, where she established herself as an embroideress and black and white illustrator. In 1906 Annie Kenney and Mrs Pankhurst visited Glasgow and stayed with the Frasers. Her father chaired their public meeting and it was here that Helen made her first speech. Shortly after this meeting she visited the London WSPU headquarters and helped at a by-election campaign. She was then asked to work as an organiser in Scotland. In 1908 Mrs Pankhurst visited Scotland announcing that the WSPU was going to use more violent tactics. Helen disagreed with this decision and resigned from the WSPU. Shortly afterwards in August 1908 she was appointed NUWSS organiser for Scotland and from 1909 worked and travelled as such until World War I. She described this work as (Moyes, 1971, 32)

"... speaking, organising by-election campaigns in England, Scotland and Wales and once a tour of Ireland, both north and south. My experiences varied from friendly audiences and cheering people to one meeting where one stone of several thrown, cut my head, my only encounter with real violence, though I had many lively meetings all over the country."

Although Helen disapproved of violent militant tactics, she admired the women using them as she felt it revealed depths of character and qualities of courage, loyalty and tenacity as well as a certain amount of dissatisfaction with contemporary society. This was probably a view held by many NUWSS members. Helen continued her political activity during the war, when she toured the United States for the NUWSS and spoke about their war effort. In 1922 she was the first woman to be adopted as a parliamentary candidate in Scotland and stood unsuccessfully twice as a National Liberal candidate. In 1939 she married and emigrated to Australia where she continued to write and campaign for women's rights.

In 1910 the Liskeard society secretary, Miss Jessie Williams, planned and executed an autumn campaign further afield. This included door-to-door canvassing in Fowey, open air meetings in Looe (encountering a little opposition), Lostwithiel and Bodmin. In December Miss Duncan, possibly another NUWSS organiser, carried out an election campaign which covered most of Cornwall including St. Ives and Penzance. It was possibly as a result of these activities that two new societies were formed the following March in Penzance and Falmouth.

In Penzance there were problems in establishing the society since members encountered local Liberal opposition, particularly from the M.P., Sir John Clifford Cory, who supported the Prime Minister in opposing women's suffrage (*CC*, March 9th, 1911). This made it difficult to work with Liberal sympathisers. Suffrage supporters threatened to resign from the local Women's Liberal Federation if he did not support the Conciliation Bill. Although a society was set up with between 40 and 50 members, this may have been responsible, together with potential members belonging to the WSPU, for the eventual lack of success in Penzance and the society being reformed the following year (*CC*, May 16th, 1912).

Elsewhere in the county, NUWSS activity was helped by the newly-formed Federation. They appointed a travelling NUWSS organiser at the beginning of 1911 to visit societies throughout Devon and Cornwall. She was Miss Alice Abadam (1856-1940), an unusual appointment, since as Elizabeth Crawford describes her, she was "a peripatetic speaker to a variety of suffrage societies" and not a member of the NUWSS (Crawford, 1999, 1).

Cornwall was perceived by the Federation as a difficult area to tackle, possibly because of the earlier success of their rival, the WSPU. At their first Annual meeting they put forward an ambitious plan. (*CC*, May 4th, 1911). They would form a society in every Cornish constituency. In order to do this an organiser was mandated to spend a week in each centre and since more speakers were needed the chosen organiser was also requested to hold speakers' classes. There is no record that this took place or that there was more activity. The main result was the formation of a branch in Falmouth. The inaugural meeting was addressed by Alice Abadam, who spoke about the Tax Resistance League (established in 1909) to a large audience which included Mr Barclay Fox and Falmouth's Mayor (*CC*, March 30th, 1911).

In August 1911 the holiday campaign intensified activity. This was due to Miss Baker's energetic tour. She addressed 32 public meetings, indoor and open air ones and enrolled numerous new members and subscribers to *Common Cause*. This tour was described enthusiastically by two contributors to *Common Cause*. Firstly (*CC*, August 31st, 1911) Maude Slater, an Exeter NUWSS member, used the headline "Work in South West: Tub Thumping in Cornwall". Secondly (*CC* September 14th, 1911), 'AWJ' (anon.) described a walk with Hatty Baker from Penzance to Mousehole on August Bank holiday. Here they distributed literature to each house and held an open air meeting at Mousehole harbour to an audience of sympathetic fishermen. AWJ obviously loved Mousehole harbour which she described as:

"That harbour! Iridescent water, quaint multi-coloured boats, scraps of coppery red canvass - all with the blue ocean behind it."

Hatty (Harriet) Baker was yet another unusual organiser for the Federation to choose. She was a founder of the newly formed Free Church League for Women's Suffrage and the only Congregationalist woman minister. She was possibly the sister of the Secretary and Treasurer of the Budleigh Salterton NUWSS. Her numerous meetings included the first suffrage meeting at St. Just, financed by Mrs Robins Bolitho. At this meeting, held at the home of Mrs Richmond, "the only 'Anti' confessed at being almost persuaded." It was here that the most westerly branch in England, Pendeen, was set up with an acting secretary, Mrs Bennett (*CC*, August 31st, 1911).

In November another tour was organised for Mrs Ethel Snowden (1881-1946), the socialist suffragist wife of Philip Snowden, Chairman of the Independent Labour Party. She was a member of the NUWSS executive committee. This tour included a successful meeting at the Drill Hall, Falmouth (*CC,* December 7th, 1911). This was a colourful affair since not only was the platform decorated in the NUWSS colours "rich red and.festoons of greenery and white chrysanthemums" but ten stewards carried bags and baskets in these colours. There was music and a large audience of suffragists, anti-suffragists, Liberals, Conservatives and Socialists, presided over by the Mayor, Alderman F.J. Bowler. The local Liberal Unionist M.P. Charles Goldman sent a message of goodwill. A resolution supporting the Conciliation Bill was sent to the Prime Minister and eighty copies of *Common Cause* sold.

In 1912 the Falmouth society organised numerous activities ranging from public meetings, fundraising by holding a Valentine's Fair and

White Elephant sale, and a canvass of municipal meetings. One of their most successful meetings was on March 14th, 1912. Despite fears of organised opposition, as a result of the WSPU window smashing campaign, the Cambridge suffragist, Mrs Clara Rackham addressed a large peaceful meeting, chaired by Colonel Vyvyan (a Vice President of the South Western Federation) at the Drill Hall (CC May 2nd, 1912). Again this was decorated in NUWSS colours, this time using laurel wreaths and arum lilies against a red background. Mrs Rackham (1875-1965) was a socialist, married to a Cambridge academic, and a leading suffragist who spoke at many public meetings around Britain. In March 1914, she returned to speak again in Cornwall, this time in St. Ives and Bodmin.

Between 1912 and 1913 the Federation appointed a series of organisers. First, Miss G. Davenport, followed by Miss Marguerite Norma-Smith, Miss Mary Fielden and finally Miss D. Walford. The latter two helped form societies in Truro and St. Ives. Miss Norma-Smith spoke at the first and particularly successful meeting in Wadebridge in May 1912 (CC May 16th, 1912). Here the main speaker was the popular Scottish suffragist, Miss Chrystal Macmillan (1871-1937). She was a member of the NUWSS executive committee, a Liberal and one of the first women to matriculate at Edinburgh University. The previous year she had attended the sixth congress of the International Woman Suffrage Alliance in Stockholm.

People apparently came to the meeting in 1912 at Wadebridge, out of curiosity and it was the main topic of conversation for several days. It was so successful that on the following day a society was formed locally by the organiser of the meeting, Mrs Emily Macmillan, who became its President.

In August Hatty Baker returned again to Cornwall and broke 'new ground' since she addressed the first suffrage meeting at the Lizard in a kitchen (Mrs Richard Jose's). Here she spoke to a crowded meeting on the benefits of women's suffrage with particular reference to the White Slave trade (CC October 3rd, 1912).

In November two well known speakers visited Cornwall (CC November 29th, 1912). The first, Mr Baillie Weaver, addressed a meeting in Falmouth. He was a member of the Men's League for Women's Suffrage, a pacifist, anti-vivisectionist and theosophist. The meeting was chaired by Mrs F.D.(Augustus) Acland, the wife of the Right Honorable Sir Francis Dyke Acland who was then Liberal M.P. for Camborne (1910-1922) and Parliamentary Under-Secretary for Foreign Affairs (1911-1915). Both supported women's suffrage and from 1912 onwards she was a Vice President of the South Western Federation and a member of the WFL. The second large meeting was held in Wadebridge and addressed by Lady Frances Balfour.

Lady Frances (1858-1931) was the daughter of the Duke of Argyle who was married to Eustace Balfour, the architect brother of Arthur Balfour, the former Conservative Prime Minister. She was, however, a Liberal, and an experienced public speaker who had campaigned for women's suffrage since the formation of the NUWSS. She was President of two Devon societies, Honiton and Sidmouth. At the meeting chaired by Dr Mabel Ramsay, the chairman of the South Western Federation, she spoke about the recently formed government divorce commission as well as why women wanted the vote. She returned to Cornwall the following year to address a meeting at Launceston.

At first, campaigning in 1913 was similar to previous years. Former visiting speakers returned to Cornwall. Falmouth and Truro continued to hold regular meetings. including one in May at Truro (CC June 6th, 1913) which was addressed by Helen Fraser, this time with two Liberal Parliamentary supporters, the Hon H.H. McClaren and Mr W.J. Mirlees.

The spring months were taken up with preparations for the major event, the Pilgrimage. Since one of the main routes began at Land's End and crossed Cornwall, this more than anything else helped to integrate the Cornish societies into the mainstream of the NUWSS. The aims of this nationwide demonstration were to prove to the public and the government that support for the cause was widespread and that the majority of suffrage supporters were peaceful. Thus it was seen as a means of counteracting the more extreme image of suffrage supporters created by the WSPU. On the more practical side the NUWSS wanted to recruit members, raise funds and hold meetings in every town and village along the eight routes, which followed the eight major roads in Britain. All eight marches took six weeks to complete and concluded with a large meeting in Hyde Park on July 26th, followed by a deputation to the Prime Minister.

The first verse of 'The Song of the Suffrage Pilgrim' (*CC* June 20th, 1913) illustrates some of these aims. It was written by Miss Tanner and set to the tune of the 'Song of the Western Man'.

'A good heart and steady mind,
  Our purpose clear in view,
And we will show our country now
  What women folk can do.
From Land's End by the blue sea coast,
  From far beyond the Tweed,
We march that all the countryside
  May know the women's need.'

The Devon and Cornwall section of the Pilgrimage was supported and financed by the South Western Federation who appointed an organiser, named variously in *Common Cause* as Miss Misick or G.C. de C. Misick. She was based in Exeter and worked together with local groups and Federation executive committee members. As elsewhere the fittest and youngest women travelled by foot or bicycle or on horseback, whilst older women travelled by car or carriage. Luggage was transported by cart or car, or as in Cornwall by a horse-drawn van decorated with NUWSS posters. The pilgrims were instructed to wear grey, white, black or blue skirts, coats or dresses. Hats were to be simple, decorated only with the NUWSS tricolour. They all wore a specially designed NUWSS badge and haversack. En route, the pilgrims stopped and held open air meetings, either in the countryside or in the small towns where they often stopped overnight, staying with local members (see Table 6). In Cornwall these were mainly addressed by Miss Helen Fraser who marched nearly all the way. Two women from Exeter NUWSS, Miss Baly and Dr Ramsay's sixty year old mother, called by *Common Cause* (August 1st, 1913) "the veteran pilgrim", walked the whole route.

Table 6. Route of the pilgrimage through Cornwall, June 1913
Source: *Common Cause*

Thursday	June 19	Land's End to Penzance
Friday	June 20	Penzance to Camborne via Hayle
Saturday	June 21	Camborne to Falmouth
Sunday	June 22	Falmouth
Monday	June 23	Falmouth to Truro
Tuesday	June 24	Truro to Bodmin
Wednesday	June 25	Bodmin to St. Austell
Thursday	June 26	St. Austell to Fowey
Friday	June 27	Fowey to Looe
Saturday	June 28	Looe to St. Germans & then by ferry to Plymouth
Sunday	June 29	Plymouth

Seven women, (*CC,* June 27th, 1913) including Miss Misick, Mrs Ramsay, Miss Baly and Miss Fraser started off from Land's End in a "large covered van with its painted head board 'Land's End to London.'" They were given a "a hearty send off" by Mrs Robins Bolitho, photographed by a *Daily Mirror* photographer and a number of men assembled and cheered them on their way." (*The Cornishman* June 26th, 1913) Along the route they leafleted houses. At the Trereife crossroads, just outside Penzance they were met by sympathisers, 20 of whom, including Mrs Bolitho and other Penzance members, joined the march. Since it was market day in Penzance they marched down the back streets. At 8 p.m. they held an open air meeting in the Pig Market addressed by Helen Fraser and Mr Dale. Here (*The Cornishman* June 26th, 1913)

'(Miss Fraser) was met with occasional outbursts by the opposition. She was so good, that in spite of the rain, the crowd increased in numbers - unfortunately in the middle of her speech some misguided but probably well-meaning person must have suggested it would be advisable to bring the platform a little further out. Miss Fraser paused to enable this to be done. The pause was fatal. The spell was broken. The hobble-de-hoy again asserted himself and received vigorous support from the boys in the "gallery". When the speaker endeavoured to pick up the broken thread of her argument she was met with constant interruption which drowned her voice. This all increased and there was a danger that the platform would be swept away in the tumult. At this point the mayor, A.E. Barnett mounted the platform - appealed to the crowd effectively and Miss Fraser continued. She was also questioned, then distributed literature and collected funds - however before this could take place - a struggle between the police and the people near the vicinity of the platform took place. The suffragists went to the home of Mrs J.B. Cornish... Miss Fraser had been kicked in the ankle.'

This was the beginning of an eventful week. The following day about a dozen pilgrims marched to Camborne, via Hayle. On the way they were met by members from St. Ives and St. Erth. They experienced some opposition. At an open air meeting in Foundry Square in Hayle their reception began quietly. Helen Fraser (*The Cornish Post* June 26th, 1913) was careful to point out that they were not members of the "Mrs Pankhurst Society and had no sympathy with methods of violence." They did however have to retreat with the help of the police when "half a dozen motor-cyclists swooped down on them," who according to the *Royal Cornwall Gazette* (June 26th) were mining students. Then, just outside Hayle while they were picnicking at Loggan's Mill, a man swore at them when he was offered a leaflet by a sixty year old woman.

At Camborne they were heckled, and as *The Cornish Post* (June 26th) described:

'Between Connor Downs and Treswithian a young motor-bike fiend (the scorching whirl-wind variety) had the bravado to snatch a satchel off the shoulder of one of the lady speakers and throw it on the road. This worried some of the party, but the leaders took it in good part. Asked if they were prepared for a shower of eggs, the lawyer's wife (probably Mrs Cornish) laughed and said "We heard that was to happen at Penzance, but it didn't. Perhaps at Camborne, we had better wear water-proofs!"'

The next day they marched to Falmouth where Helen Fraser together with Mrs Macmillan addressed a crowd of about 2,000, including the deputy mayor, at Falmouth on the recreation ground. This time the crowd rushed them, but with the help of the police, they were able to evade the crowd. After resting for a day in Falmouth they proceeded to Truro.

At Truro comments reported by the *Royal Cornwall Gazette* (June 26th) were also antagonistic.

'"They ought to be burned" exclaimed a well known tradesman; Youth "Down with the women"; "They ought to be shot", said a woman viewing them.'

The next day they proceeded to Bodmin, where at another open air meeting (*VW* July 11th, 1913), the mayor appealed for a "sympathetic hearing throughout Cornwall."

The following day they decided not to hold a meeting at St. Austell, but stopped there overnight. The next day, Helen Fraser was met by the mayor at Fowey. Here their meeting was transferred from the quay to the town hall, because there was such a large crowd. At Looe the crowd was once more antagonistic. In contrast, on the final day in Cornwall at St. Germans (*CC* July 4th, 1913), "they had a delightful village meeting, collecting many names of Friends and good wishes." Finally they took the ferry across the Tamar to Plymouth where the following day they held a successful public meeting, and recruited over 120 'Friends' (*CC* July 4th, 1913). Incidentally 'Friends' were supporters who pledged their support by signing a card but did not have to pay a subscription. They were then supplied with suffrage literature. The scheme was launched in 1912 in order to specifically recruit working class women.

It is interesting that *Common Cause* (July 4th) commented on the Cornish part of the Pilgrimage enthusiastically, ignoring the antagonism with which the pilgrims were met. Pilgrims encountered hostility not only in Cornwall but elsewhere. This hostility was probably because the Pilgrimage coincided with the the pillar box and arson campaigns which were widely and unsympathetically reported

pledge his support for women's suffrage until he was elected. The following month a new organiser, Miss Frost worked in Cornwall (*CC* July 3rd). She, together with Mrs Smart, a South Western Federation press secretary, claimed to speak at the first suffrage meeting held at Helston (in fact early speakers had held meetings here in the 1870s). She then spent a week in Newquay where she explained NUWSS policy to the new society (*CC* August 7th, 1914). Finally just before the declaration of war, two meetings took place in Truro and Launceston.

As this account demonstrates the Cornish societies relied a great deal on the South Western Federation, since they supplied organisers who often addressed and held public meetings in the more isolated areas. The Federation also provided them with links to other suffrage societies and kept them in touch with the NUWSS nationally.

Federations were formed in 1909 in response to the growth and increasing demands on local suffrage societies. By 1912 they existed all over Britain. They were expected not only to co-ordinate local societies but also to form new societies and were given powers to run local campaigns. The Federation, like the rest of the NUWSS had an annually elected executive committee that included a secretary, treasurer, chairman as well as President and a galaxy of Vice Presidents (see Table 7). The South Western Federation was dominated by Devon women, probably because they had many more societies than Cornwall. It held quarterly executive committee meetings rotating these in different towns in both counties. Here they planned and carried out policies decided on at their annual meetings and by the NUWSS executive committee. Their income was derived from individual societies subscribing a minimum fee of 10/- per annum. This money paid for an organiser. In line with NUWSS policy they published annual reports, although unfortunately only one South Western Federation report (1914) has survived.

Table 7. The South Western Federation Executive Committee, 1911-1915
(Compiled from various sources and incomplete)

President:
| 1911-1912 | Mrs Wyndham Knight-Bruce (Newton Abbott) |
| 1912-1915 | Lady Courtney of Penwith |

Vice Presidents:
1912-	Mrs Frances Dyke (Margaret) Acland (Exeter)
1912-1915	The Lady Rosalind Northcote (Exeter)
	Sir Robert Newman, Bart
1914-1915	Mrs Robins (Augusta) Bolitho (Penzance)
	Mrs Herman (Liskeard)
	Col Courtney Vyvyan, C.B. (Cornwall)

Chairman:
1910-1913	Dr. Mabel Ramsay (Plymouth)
1913-1914	Mrs Fletcher (Exeter)
1914-1915	Mrs Wyndham Knight-Bruce (Newton Abbott)

Hon. Secretary:
1910-1913	Mrs Penry (Exeter)
	Mrs M.E. Wilcocks, B.A. (Exeter)
1913-1915	Mrs Mattieson, M.A. (Budleigh Salterton)

Treasurer:
1910-1913	Mrs Ross (Exeter)
1913-1914	Mrs Thomas (Sidmouth)
1914-1915	Mrs Holmes (Exeter)

Hon. Press Secretary:
| 1914-1915 | Miss Baly (Exeter) and |
| | Mrs Smart (Mullion) |

The South Western Federation began life with ten societies. By the end of 1911 this had increased to 17 and by the outbreak of the First

73

World War to 26. In February 1911 the Federation was in a position to pay an organiser. The first two made their headquarters in Plymouth. In November 1911, Eleanor Rathbone, a leading member of the NUWSS executive committee, contributed £100 towards funds for the organiser, since the majority of societies had little money to contribute towards this (*CC* November 9th, 1911). In 1912 the headquarters moved from Plymouth to Exeter, where it remained until at least 1914.

So far I have described some of the speakers and organisers, but it would also be interesting to know details concerning the local members. Although numerically local NUWSS membership was known at least by 1914, it is difficult to generalise as to who the members actually were, since apart from the names of local committee members, I have found little additional information. Certainly they included both women and men. From the sketchy details, outlined below, it seems that the majority of activists in Falmouth, Penzance and Wadebridge were middle class women.

Falmouth was dominated by yet another generation of the Fox family and their friends. The Vice President of the Falmouth society was Mrs Ellen Fox (1846-?), the daughter of Francis and Ellen Bassett, from Leighton Buzzard. In 1867 Ellen married Robert Fox and they had two daughters and a son. In the *Women's Who's Who* (1913) she declared her interests, "as all social reforms." She was a Vice President of the Parish Nursing Association and a committee member of the Elizabeth Barclay Home for the Care of Feeble-minded Girls. Her daughter, Naomi (1886-?), secretary of Falmouth NUWSS, lived with her mother at Fox Grove Hill. She was also a member of various local philanthropic societies such as the Central Guild of Help and the Earles Retreat Almshouses.

More interestingly Ellen Fox was a member of the London Society for Women's Suffrage and the Friends' League for Women's Suffrage, both of which must have provided her and Falmouth with useful national contacts. Her cousin Olivia (1868-?), the daughter of Robert and Blanche Fox was an NUWSS member and a Poor Law Guardian. Another Vice President and friend, Julia Hawke Genn (1858-?) was

President of the pro-suffrage Falmouth Women's Liberal Association. The second of their friends, the society's treasurer, was Mrs Isabel Stephens, the daughter of Robert Sturge, a Bristol Quaker and suffrage supporter. In 1890 she married John Gilbert Stephens, the owner of John Stephens and Son Ltd, rope manufacturers. John was a magistrate and also an active suffrage supporter.

A little is known about one of the main supporters in Penzance. Their secretary (1913-1915), was Margaret Cornish, Mrs J.B. Cornish. She was the daughter of Rev. William Hadow and Mary Lang Cornish who lived in South Cerney, Gloucestershire. They had six children. Her younger sister was Grace Hadow (1875-1939), a leading Oxford suffragist and secretary of Cirencester NUWSS. In Grace's biography by Helena Deneka (1946) a few details can be gleaned about Margaret. She was mainly educated at home and in her teens went to stay with her uncle, Archdeacon Cornish, vicar of Kenwyn and later Bishop of St. Germans. Here she met her future husband John, a cousin and they were married in 1894. They lived at 4, Clarence Place, Penzance. He was a Penzance solicitor and carried out all the legal work for the Newlyn Art Gallery as well as being its treasurer for thirty years. According to Grace Hadow "he was a passionate yachtsman" and introduced Grace to the Cornish coast (Deneke 1946, 23). Grace and her mother spent summers between 1909 and 1914 in Penzance, presumably staying with her sister. Another member of the Penzance society was Mrs Robins (Augusta Jane) Bolitho, nee Wilson. She came from Yorkshire. In 1870 she married Thomas Robins Bolitho, (1840-1925) a wealthy banker, County Councillor, magistrate, master of the local fox hounds and owner of Trengwainton House, near Penzance. After the war in 1920 she was appointed the first woman magistrate in Cornwall.

The President of the St. Ives NUWSS, Mrs Augusta Lindner (1859-?), was the daughter of the Royal Academician, F.M. Smith. In 1896 she came to St. Ives to study painting under Julius Olsen. Here she met her husband Moffat Lindner, a painter, President of the St. Ives Arts' Club and a member of the New English Art Club, London. She was a landscape and flower painter. Her portrait was painted by various artists including Phillip Wilson Steer in 1900, Marianne Stokes and Frances Hodgkins.

In Wadebridge, the President and founder of the society was Mrs Emily Macmillan, nee Symons. In 1909 she married Captain James Melrose Macmillan, (1875-?) a solicitor and partner of her father's firm (later R.J.E. Symons and Macmillan), magistrate and clerk to the Wadebridge Petty Sessions. They lived at Trehare Cottage, Polzeath. She was possibly the sister of Helen Symons, the Wadebridge NUWSS secretary, who lived at Atlantic House, Polzeath.

Compared with the WSPU, there were more married women amongst the NUWSS activists. The NUWSS campaign tended to rely more on local supporters. Their organisers, apart from Helen Fraser are however far less visible and do not have the glamour of the WSPU ones. In contrast the NUWSS speakers come from a more varied backgrounds, since they were not just confined to NUWSS members but came from a variety of other suffrage organisations.

The account also illustrates that to begin with the NUWSS campaign was not as intense as the WSPU one. Indeed, in spite of the larger number of established societies, it was only intensive during periods when there was a specific campaign. These were all like the WSPU ones, in effect recruitment drives. Both groups however were remarkably similar in their campaigning techniques, relying on recruiting support through mainly holding public meetings, leafleting and selling copies of their journals.

Thus in conclusion the second phase of the suffrage campaign was in many respects similar to the campaign in the rest of England, although it lacked any militant action which, for example, dominated nearby Wales. Here the campaign was dominated by the WSPU's militancy that came into conflict with the nationalist movement, targeting Lloyd George, Chancellor of Exchequer and the National Eisteddfod. The NUWSS attempted to recruit Welsh members by translating suffrage literature into Welsh and members wore Welsh costume at national demonstrations.

In Cornwall, as far as I can ascertain, the Cornish revival movement does not play a role in the suffrage movement at all. The one factor that both areas had in common was that politically they were solidly Liberal, and that Liberal candidates and M.P.s were periodically lobbied by the various suffrage groups.

However, what does make the Cornish campaign unique, was the lack of militant campaigns in 1913 and 1914. This lack may have been accounted for by the influence of Emmeline Pethick Lawrence, although no branch of the United Suffragists existed in Cornwall and militancy in the form of the destruction of property seems never to have been discussed. What is also surprising is the lack of NUWSS rancour expressed against the WSPU, particularly since by 1912 the NUWSS nationally and publicly had disassociated itself from the WSPU. It is also astonishing that both organisations managed to coexist in Truro and Falmouth where they both held large meetings, often on consecutive days, which must have confused the general public. Thus the overall impression of this second phase of the campaign is that it was run on a highly conventional pressure group basis, by conventional middle class women.

Epilogue

By 1914 both the NUWSS and the WSPU were well established in Cornwall. However the advent of the First World War in August, that year put an end to WSPU activity which as elsewhere, with the exception of the larger provincial cities, disappeared. Only two Cornish members are recorded as remaining staunch supporters of the WSPU's policy of supporting the government, in an ultra- patriotic way (another story). In a letter to *The Suffragette* (April 1915) Mrs Powell wrote that she and her daughter would continue to promote the journal in Penzance and send a donation to the WSPU. Cornish NUWSS societies however survived until at least 1918, although according to the NUWSS Annual Reports, by 1916, the South Western Federation seems to have disappeared. The local branches of the NUWSS and the Federation supported the war effort. In this, they followed NUWSS policy and although there were divisions nationally, with the majority supporting the war effort and a minority opposing the war, there is no record of these divisions in Cornwall.

From my reading of the suffrage societies' annual reports and the South Western Federation Report I have managed to put together a brief picture of suffrage activity during this period. It is a period where much more research is needed. However like other areas of Britain, all women's lives were influenced by the war, either directly or indirectly.

At the outbreak of war, as a result of the German invasion of Belgium, there was an influx of Belgian refugees to Britain. The NUWSS helped to look after some of these and in Cornwall, the Truro and St. Ives societies were responsible for these refugees' welfare and collecting money for them. Other activities were less demanding. For example, the Launceston society continued to hold meetings fortnightly for members and 'Friends' on issues concerned with women and children and how the War would affect them. In Wadebridge a school was started for mothers, presumably for poor women, in order to help them cope with the war. Individual members also worked locally in hospitals and for the Red Cross. Others joined local authority relief committees. As the 1914 South Western Federation Report states members also participated in other NUWSS wartime schemes.

78

For example, between 1914 and 1915, members of the Falmouth, Torquay and Plymouth societies worked together with

'the National Union of Women Workers in organising Women Patrols, and this work of helping young and frivolous girls has been appreciated by the military and by the police. In connexion with this work, it is most useful to have girls' clubs where girls can invite their men friends, such clubs have been established in Falmouth, Exmouth and Budleigh Salterton; in Falmouth it has been combined with a washing and mending scheme for the troops in the town.'

Local societies, again in line with NUWSS policy, raised money for the NUWSS Scottish Women's Hospital for Foreign Service, established by Dr. Elsie Inglis, a Scottish NUWSS member in 1914. These hospitals were situated in the main war zones and were financed and staffed by women, mainly NUWSS members. In Cornwall, for example, St. Ives NUWSS raised £19 in 1916. A former organiser, Miss Frost, raised £500 for a 'Cornish Women's Ambulance' for these hospitals and hoped to use her skill as a driver to drive this vehicle in France. In October 1914 Dr Mabel Ramsay worked in a hospital in Antwerp, from which she eventually had to escape. She then went on to work in a hospital in Cherbourg.

In 1916 a similar scheme to the Scottish Hospitals, was organised in Russia by the NUWSS. This was the Millicent Fawcett Hospital Units, mainly maternity units. Both Launceston and Falmouth raised money for them, whilst some individual members such as Mrs Robins Bolitho and her husband donated money to both schemes.

Many historians have argued that it was this war work that finally gained women over the age of thirty the vote in 1918. Certainly suffragists were able to make good use of their organisational skills in supporting the war. They, apart from the WSPU, also continued to campaign for women's suffrage and lobbied the Speaker's Electoral Reform Committee, set up by the new Prime Minister, Lloyd George in October 1916. In January 1917 the Committee reported its findings and recommended that women householders and wives of householders over the age of thirty should be given the vote in all national and local government elections. Finally in February 1918 the

Representation of the People Act was passed. This was followed by the Eligibility of Women Act which allowed women to stand at the General Election. Seventeen women stood as candidates, including Emmeline Pethick Lawrence, who stood for the Labour Party. Only one woman was successful, Constance Markiewiez, a Sinn Fein candidate who refused to take her seat. The first woman to take a seat was the American born, Lady Astor, who was elected in a by-election in 1919 as Conservative M.P. for Plymouth, her husband's former seat, before he inherited his peerage.

By 1918 however the story of women's suffrage was still not complete. Nationally the NUWSS reformed itself in 1919 to become the National Union for Equal Citizenship (NUSEC), with a new President, Eleanor Rathbone. NUSEC attempted to translate the suffrage goals into practical reality for as many people as possible, by putting pressure on Parliament to legislate for equal pay, the right of married women for employment and taxation, equal moral standards for divorce, family allowances and the endowment of motherhood. They also continued to campaign for the extension of suffrage to the women excluded in the 1918 Act and this was finally achieved in 1928.

In Cornwall, as elsewhere, women slowly made inroads into public life. For example in 1920 the first Cornish woman magistrate was appointed, Mrs Robins Bolitho. She was followed by seven more, none of who appear to have been suffrage supporters. In 1928 the first woman M.P. for a Cornish constituency was elected for St. Ives. This was the Liberal Mrs Hilda Runciman, the wife of Walter Runciman, a former cabinet minister who had lost his seat. The campaign and election were complicated in that the voters were offered two candidates for the price of one. In the 1929 General Election Hilda Runciman withdrew so that her husband could stand for St. Ives. She stood for Tavistock which she lost, whilst her husband was successfully elected.

Writing an account of local history rather than a national one has, I hope, produced an added dimension to the history of the suffrage struggle. It illustrates how this one issue touched and influenced many people's lives. Cornish women and men, like individuals elsewhere in

Britain, made a vital contribution to this campaign, since without their unremitting perseverance and patience, it would have taken much longer for women to participate fully in the democratic process.

Writing a history of the Cornish movement has also at times been frustrating. Their activities were certainly well recorded, but it has been difficult to trace biographical details about the majority of the Cornish supporters and thus on the whole they remain a rather anonymous group. Nevertheless they all did in some way help women to gain the vote in 1918 and 1928, which in turn helped to bring about major political, social and economic changes for women.

During both phases of the campaign, however, it is noticeable that in spite of the efforts of the visiting speakers, organisers and the local activists, the movement was predominantly centred in the towns where there was a stable, politicised middle class. This was in spite of the efforts made by campaigners to reach the population in the mining and rural communities. This can be partially explained by the poverty in these areas and the high levels of emigration particularly from the mining villages. An additional factor which might have accounted for their lack of interest is that they would not have received any benefits from the campaign. This was because the main thrust of the suffrage movement until the First World War, was to campaign for the vote on the same basis as men, which was still based on property rights. This would have meant that few working class women would have been able to vote in elections.

Even though this history is incomplete, I hope that it will encourage future historians to redress the balance of women's suffrage and continue to 'rediscover' suffrage history outside London. It is also important for historians to recognise that women in Cornwall have contributed a great deal to this county's history. The sources exist and are just waiting to be discovered. As Sandra Holton says (1996, 249):
'Historical knowledge must always remain provisional, for new evidence, new ways of looking at evidence, may alter what we see, produce new interpretations, and make possible some fresh story-telling.'

BIBLIOGRAPHY

(The literature about the women's suffrage campaign in general is enormous. I have therefore only included the main primary sources and a selection of books that have been useful for researching the Cornish suffrage movement.)

PRIMARY SOURCES

BODLEIAN LIBRARY, OXFORD
National Society for Women's Suffrage Society Central Committee Annual Report 1884-1897
Declaration in Favour of Women's Suffrage 1889
National Union of Women's Suffrage Societies: Central and East of England Society for Women's Suffrage Annual Report 1898-1902
National Union of Women's Suffrage Societies West of England Federation Annual Report 1912-1913

DYRHAM HOUSE, Gloucestershire (National Trust)
Mary Blathwayt Diaries. 1906-1914

FAWCETT LIBRARY, GUILDHALL UNIVERSITY, LONDON
National Union of Women's Suffrage Societies Annual Report 1904-1918 (incomplete)
National Union of Women's Suffrage Societies, South Western Federation Annual Report 1914-1915
National Women's Social and Political Union, Annual Report 1907-1914

CONTEMPORARY JOURNALS
The Anti-Suffrage Review
Common Cause
The Englishwoman's Review
The Suffragette
The Vote
The Women's Suffrage Journal
Votes for Women

LOCAL NEWPAPERS
Cornish Post and Morning News
Cornishman

Royal Cornwall Gazette
St. Ives Weekly Summary
West Briton

BOOKS

Atkinson, Diane (1996) *The Suffragettes in Pictures*. Stroud: Sutton Publishing.

Banks, Olive (1986) *Becoming a Feminist: the Social Origins of 'First-wave' Feminism*. Brighton; Wheatsheaf Books.

Volume One, 1800-1930 The Biographical Dictionary of British Feminists (1985), Brighton: Wheatsheaf Books.

Volume Two: a Supplement, 1900-1945 The Biographical Dictionary of British Feminists (1990), Hemel Hempstead: Wheatsheaf Books.

Bennett, Alan (1987) *Cornwall: Through the mid-Nineteenth Century*. Southampton: Kingfisher Railway Productions.

Blackburn, Helen (1902) *Women's Suffrage: a Record of the Women's Suffrage Movement in the British Isles*. London: S.Norgate.

_____(1881) *A Handbook for Women Engaged in Social and Political Work*. Bristol: J.W. Arrowsmith.

Bolt, Christine (1993) *The Women's Movements in the United States and Britain from the 1790s to the 1930s*. Hemel Hempstead: Harvester Wheatsheaf.

Brett, R.L., ed. (1979) *Barclay Fox's Journal*. London: Hyman.

Caine, Barbara (1986) *Destined to be Wives, the Sisters of Beatrice Webb*. Oxford: Clarendon Press.

Channon, Joyce, ed. (1987) *St. Ives Weekly Summary, 1889-1910*. Cornwall: St. Ives Printing & Publishing Company.

Cherry, Deborah (1995) *Painting Women: Victorian Women Artists*. London & New York: Routledge.

Clarke, Jennifer (1987) *Exploring the West Country. A Woman's Guide*. London:Virago Press.

Crawford, Elizabeth (1999) *The Women's Suffrage Movement. A Reference Guide, 1866-1928*. London: University College London Press.

Daniell,S (1989) *Victorian Cornwall*. Penryn,Cornwall: Tor Mark Press.

Dobbie, B.M. Willmott (1979) *A Nest of Suffragettes in Somerset*, Eagle House, Batheaston. Bath: The Batheaston Society.

Fawcett, Millicent Garrett (1912) *Women's Suffrage: a Short History of a Great Movement*. London: E.C.Jack.

Fulford, Roger (1958) *Votes for Women*. London: Faber & Faber.

Gates, G. Evelyn, ed. (1924) *Woman's Year Book, 1923-1924*. London: Women Publishers Ltd.

Guthrie, A. (1994) *Cornwall in the Age of Steam*. Padstow: Tabb House.

Hardie, Melissa (1995) *100 Years in Newlyn: Diary of a Gallery*. Penzance: The Patten Press.

Hirsch, Pam (1998) *Barbara Leigh Smith Bodichon 1827-1891, Feminist, Artist and Rebel*. London: Chatto & Windus.

Hollis, Patricia (1987) *Ladies Elect: Women in Local Government, 1865-1914*. Oxford University Press.

Holton, Sandra (1986) *Feminism and Democracy: Women's Suffrage and Reform Politics in Britain, 1900- 1918*. Cambridge University Press.

_____(1996) *Suffrage Days: Stories from the Women's Suffrage Movement*. London & New York: Routledge.

John, Angela V, ed. (1991) *Our Mothers' Land. Chapters in Welsh Women's History, 1830-1939*. Cardiff: University of Wales Press.

Kamm, Josephine (1966) *Rapiers and Battleaxes: the Women's Movement and its Aftermath*. London: George Allen & Unwin.

Kelly's Directory of Cornwall. (Editions between 1885-1930)

Kenney, Annie (1924) *Memories of a Militant*. London: E. Arnold.

Kent, Alan (1998) *'Wives, Mothers and Sisters': Feminism, Literature and Women Writers in Cornwall*. Penzance: The Hypatia Trust

Kraditor, A (1981) *The Ideas of the Woman Suffrage Movement, 1890-1920*. New York: W.W.Norton.

Lacey, Ann Candida , ed. (1986) *Barbara Leigh Smith Bodichon and the Langham Place Group*. London: Routledge & Kegan Paul.

Levine, Philippa (1987) *Victorian Feminism, 1850-1900*. London: Hutchinson.

Lewis, Jane, ed. (1987) *Before the Vote was Won: Arguments for and against Women's Suffrage, 1864-1895*. London: Routledge & Kegan Paul.

Liddington, Jill, Norris, Jill (1978) *One Hand Tied Behind Us: the Rise of the Women's Suffrage Movement*. London: Virago.

Mackenzie, Midge (1988 repr. of 1975) *Shoulder to Shoulder*. New York: Random House.

Marcus, Jane, ed. (1987) *Suffrage and the Pankhursts*. London: Routledge & Kegan Paul.

Mason, Bertha (1912) *The Story of the Women's Suffrage Movement*. London: Sherratt & Hughes.

Metcalfe, A.E (1917) *Women's Effort: a Chronicle of British Women's Fifty Years' Struggle for Citizenship, 1865-1914*. Oxford: B.H. Blackwell.

Mitchell, Susie (1977) *Recollections of Lamorna*. Penzance: Headland Printers Ltd.

Monk, Wendy, ed. (1972) *The Journals of Caroline Fox, 1835-1871*. London: Elek Books.

Morgan, David (1975) *Suffragists and Liberals: the Politics of Women's Suffrage in Britain*. Oxford: Basil Blackwell.

Moyes, Helen (1971) *A Woman in a Man's World*. Sydney, Australia: Alpha Books.

Neville, David (1998) *To make their Mark. The Women's Suffrage Movement in the North East of England, 1900-1914*. Newcastle upon Tyne: History Workshop Trust/North East Labour History Centre for Northern Studies, University of Northumbria.

Oldfield, Sybil (1989) *Women Against the Iron Fist Alternatives to Militarism 1900-1918*. Oxford: Basil Blackwell.

Orme, Nicholas, ed. (1991) *Unity and Variety: a History of the Church in Devon and Cornwall*. Exeter Studies in History, Number 20, University of Exeter Press.

Palmer, June, ed. (1994) *Edwardian Truro*. Truro: Local History Monographs.

Pankhurst, Christabel (1987) *Unshackled: the Story of How We Won the Vote*. (1959) London: Cresset Women's Voices.

Pankhurst, Emmeline (1914) *My Own Story*. (Written by Reta Childe Dorr) London: Eveleigh Nash.

Pankhurst, Sylvia (1978, repr of 1931) *The Suffragette Movement*. London: Virago.

Payton, Philip (1992) *The Making of Modern Cornwall: Historical Experience and the Persistence of Difference*. Redruth: Dyllansow Truran.

_____(1996) *Cornwall*. Fowey, Cornwall: Alexander Associates.

_____Ed. (1993) *Cornwall since the War: the Contemporary History of a European Region*. Redruth: Institute of Cornish Studies.

Pethick Lawrence, Emmeline (1938) *My Part in a Changing World*. London: Gollancz.

Pethick Lawrence, Frederick (1943) *Fate has been kind*. London: Hutchinson.

Probert, John Charles (1966) *Primitive Methodism in Cornwall*. Cornish Methodist Historical Association.

Pugh, Martin (1995) *Votes for Women in England, 1865-1928*. London: Historical association.

_____ (1980) *Women's Suffrage in Britain, 1867-1928*. London: Historical Association.

Raeburn, Antonia (1973) *Militant Suffragettes*. London: Michael Joseph.

Ramelson, Marion (1972) *The Petticoat Rebellion: a Century of Struggle for Women's Rights*. London: Lawrence & Wishart.

Rosen, Andrew (1974) *Rise up Women! The Militant Campaign of the Women's Social and Political Union, 1903-1914.* London: Routledge & Kegan Paul.

Rubenstein, David (1986) *Before the Suffragettes: Women's Emancipation in the 1890s.* Brighton: Harvester Press.

Shiman, Lilian Lewis (1992) *Women and Leadership in Nineteenth Century England.* London: Macmillan.

Strachey, Ray (1978 repr of 1928) *The Cause: a Short History of the Women's Movement in Great Britain.* London: Virago.

The Suffrage Annual and the *Women's Who's Who.* London: Stanley Paul,1913

Tickner, Lisa (1989) *The Spectacle of Women: Imagery of the Suffrage Campaign.* London: Chatto & Windus.

Tod, Robert J.N. (1980) *Caroline Fox. Quaker Blue Stocking, 1819-1971.* York: William Sessions Ltd.

Wallace, Catherine, ed.(1996) *Women Artists in Cornwall, 1880-1940.* Exhibition catalogue: Falmouth Town Council.

Whetter, J.C.A. (1981) *The History of Falmouth.* Redruth: Dyllansow Truran.

Whybrow, Marion (1994) *St. Ives, 1883-1993. Portrait of an Art Colony.* Woodbridge,Suffolk: The Antique Collectors' Club Ltd.

UNPUBLISHED THESES
Bradley, Katherine (1997) 'Faith, Perseverance and Patience: the History of the Oxford Suffrage and Anti-Suffrage Movements, 1870-1930' D.Phil. dissertation, Oxford Brookes University.

Walker, Linda (1984) 'The Women's Movement in England in the Late Nineteenth and Early Twentieth Century.' D,Phil. dissertation, University of Manchester.

MODERN ARTICLES
Deacon, Bernard (1992) 'Conybeare for Ever.' *In Old Redruth.* Redruth Old Cornwall Society , pp. 37-43.

Hirshfield, Claire (1990) 'Fractured Faith: Liberal Party Women and the Suffrage Issue in Britain, 1892-1914.' *Gender and History 2*,2, pp. 173-197.

Holton, Sandra Stanley (1992) 'The Suffragist and the 'Average Woman'.' *Women's History Review 1*,1, pp. 9-24.

_____(1996) 'Silk Dresses and Lavender Kid Gloves: the Wayward Career of Jessie Craigen, Working Suffragist.' *Women's History Review 6*, pp, 129-150.

John, Angela V.(1995) "A Draft of Fresh Air': Women's Suffrage, the Welsh and London.' *Proceedings of the Honourable Society of Cymmrodorian* , pp. 81-93.

86

Liddington, Jill (1977) 'Rediscovering Suffrage History.' *History Workshop 4*, Autumn, pp. 192-202.

Tregidga, Garry (1997) 'The Politics of the Celto-Cornish Revival, 1886-1939.' *Cornish Studies 5*, pp. 125-150.

Index of names referenced in main text

(Each forthcoming addition to *The Hypatia Notebooks* will include an index of people referenced, and the cumulative index resulting will be published at intervals, thereby assisting in the formation of the Archive of Cornish history which the Elizabeth Treffry Cornish Collection houses. Indices do not always list names used only once in a text, but in relation to this virtually uncharted research territory, it was considered useful for family historians and others to have a complete list of those contemporary people found in the records.)